Writers of the Indian Diaspora

edited by

R.K. DHAWAN

PRESTIGE

Published by
PRESTIGE BOOKS
3/28, East Patel Nagar
New Delhi 110 008
e-mail: prestigebooks@greatindian.com

ISBN: 81-7551-111-7

Rs. 500
Prestige Books International

Composed by Vivek Mathur, Delhi 110 006 Ph. 3981867
Printed at Chaman Offset Press, New Delhi 110 002

Contents

Stephen Gill

Salman Rushdie

Jhumpa Lahiri

Manorama Mathai

Meena Alexander

Contributors

P. BALASWAMY	Pondicherry University Pondicherry
URBASHI BARAT	R.D. University Jabalpur
SEEMA BHADURI	Nasik Maharashtra
NEERJA CHAND	Ram Lal Anand College University of Delhi
MADHOO KAMARA	Durga Mahavidyalaya Raipur
JOEL KUORTTI	University of Tampere Finland
JYOTI MISHRA	Raipur Chhattisgarh
A.K. MUKHERJEE	Government College Bhawanipatna
D.K. PABBY	Ram Lal Anand College University of Delhi
DAVID MYERS	Central Queensland University Rockhampton
MITALI DE SARKAR	Res. Sch., Indian School of Mines Dhanbad
R.K. SINGH	Indian School of Mines Dhanbad
PRADEEP TRIKHA	Dayanand College Ajmer

Stephen Gill: A Search for Elysium

R.K. SINGH and MITALI DE SARKAR

I was ever free
a bird
diamond unrevealed[1]

Like Shiv K. Kumar, Keki N. Daruwalla and Arvind Krishna Mehrotra (born in Lahore), Stephen Gill was born in Pakistan (Sialkot) and speaks Punjabi, Urdu and English alongwith some other languages. All these poets stayed in different parts of the country, and like several pominent authors, Bharati Mukherjee, Uma Parameswaran, Rohinton Mistry, to name a few, Stephen Gill migrated to Canada in search of better economic prospects though it could ultimately turn out to be a struggle to discover his own identity in a hostile environment.

Gill is spiritually unable to sever his cultural and historical links with India. Reading his verses, one finds his Indian self seeking a voice in a new land; all his thought processes, his recollections of childhood or schooling, are Indian; his roots are Indian even as the world he presents—the social norms and standards and values—are neither fully Indian nor Western, these are rather international. His concerns are human just as he seems to have absorbed the elements of foreign cultures into his culture and his contexts increasingly become global. Perhaps, his cross-cultural experiences enrich his creative sensibility even as he finds himself a foreigner in his adoptive country and a stranger in his homeland.

Caught between two cultures, Indian and Canadian, he puts up with culture shock and adjustment conflicts, something every expatriate faces:

> In the valley of terror
> my bones crack,
> shooting pains of insecurity,
> while the pride of my ego
> shamelessly mocks my nakedness.[2]

He feels like a "deer lost in the jungle" and expresses his dismay:

> Often I have to caress
> even those thorns
> which knowingly pierce
> my feet[3]

He tries to bring some desperate fragments of experience into significant wholes, builds meaning out of confusion, laying things bare to those of his countrymen who cannot see them, making them aware of another truth. He seems to ironically challenge the mainstream Canadian poets who are sceptic about the immigrant Canadian poets like him:

> I wish I could capture you
> in the rainbows of my pen; but
> I am not a poet so skilled! (*FOT*, 88)

Stephen Gill sounds struggling for his identity in the country of adoption just as he looks to his old country (India) for appreciation:

> For you
> often I have tried to write,
> but alas:
> many more wounds exist
> than love's wound. (*FOT*, 84)

Though Stephen Gill is not a Canadian by birth and his sensibility is essentially international, his works add to ethnic pluralism of Canada. His poetry incorporates native consciousness and offers an international perspective from a Canadian centrality which is essentially multiracial and multicultural:

> Thy land and life
> and springs,
> thy summer and fall
> and skies
> and joyful birds—
> delight-giving sights—
> breathe a new life in me.[4]

Yet, reading his poems, novels and stories, one experiences an immigrant-consciousness at work: there is a conflict between his native Indian ethos and forces of marginal existence, nagging inconveniences, and foreign dominance in the country of his adoption. The poet evolves through raw socio-cultural pressure, barriers of race, religion, colour and nationality making creative writing a survival process, a process of coping with the uncertanities of the new environmentt, new social structure, new values, new politics and new relations.

He suffers changes, swift and fundamental, shaking even the most basic human conditions; the complexity, diversity and rapid pace of change makes him appear a stranger in his own eyes, away from his own familiar society, often leaving him nostalgic. Faced with an unrecognised life, monotony, and uncertainty, he turns an immigrant in time and voyages into the future, sometimes with an idealist tinge. Real failures and disappointments to achieve money, status, power, and success in a country where he hoped to get them forces him to cope with his surroundings and probe aspects of Canadian life, sometimes as a Canadian and sometimes as an immigrant Indian—the two psyches ever in action in his mind.

The conflict between his loyalty to the old land—the land he has come from—and the new land—his adoptive country, his willingness to accept the new geophysical setting and the resistance or unconcealed hostility of the host society leave indelible impression in his thought process. The poet is ever indignant of 'xenophobic' nationalists whom he calls "sinking vultures" and "smiling shylocks" that "rest in rusted tombs."

Bewitched by the magic of Canada, the poet voyages to this new land, which was unknown, untravelled, unexploited and so intriguing in the beginning. It could possibly have provided a challenge, a new motivating force to live his life by. But the unsettling experience of racial discrimination makes him feel more around himself. Once again, he makes an assessment of his status as a newcomer to Canada, as an individual, and as a human being, "caught at the honeycombed crossroads" of "divided humanity" :

> In the pots of patriotism
> poisons are often prepared
> to kill the lily of peace.[5]

His creative exercises reflect adjustment pangs of an immigrant who has lived through and survived against the hostility generated mainly out of uncosmopolitan profile of his so-called cosmopolitan surroundings. The range of emotions and sentiments experienced by Gill is common to most of the unfairly treated immigrants. Supercilious attitude of the natives, hurtful insults and motivated racial assaults cripple them both physically and psychologically and, as a reaction to the feelings of hurt, they take recourse to voicing their protest through the medium of writing. Gill's writing is no exception, he vehemently protests—often with a touch of desolation—against the demons of bigotries: "life will not be the same/because the night of racial predudice/chews peace/in the jaws of endless depth." (*SFH*, 48)

Since Gill has not lived his formative years in Canada nor grown in its landscapes that could speak to him directly—he migrated there as a grown-up man—he creates in terms of those cultural images that he feels perfectly at home with. The luxuriant new landscape of Canada makes him nostalgic about the villages and rivers of the motherland he experienced as a child.

There is a lurking feeling in that he is not able to love the new country as much as he loves his old country of birth. There is this element of distance which is always present both in his poetry and fiction. This is not necessarily a negative element but rather one of regret, because he seems to recognise the new evironment as worthy of being his own, yet it is not. Hence the tension, a feeling of belonging and not belonging.

His sensibility is constantly in interaction with the new locale, transmuting his experiences with the sort of creative tension every writer feels, articulating his or her inward growth. In fact, his becoming a Canadian citizen heightens his awareness of time and change: of the self isolated from others, of alienation, of the need to adapt to the present:

> In a cabin of inaction
> built with beams of silence
> often I long to slumber
> on a couch
> with no flesh of worries.
>
> For me
> soft drops of harmony
> shall produce a lullaby
> from the notes of now. (*SFH*, 19)

In this he is similar to several contemporary writers who blend their native tradition and the tradition of their country of adoption into a personal style and manner with all its awkwardness at times—trite imagery and expression, and sentimentality and weak emotional, verbal or technical interest. Sometimes, the poet reminds one of Alamgir Hashmi, a Pakistani poet born in Lahore.

Despite being in the process of adjustment with his surroundings, he demonstrates a sense of subtle nebulous links that are latent within; he expresses several inarticulate feelings and unrealised emotions against a new perspective. We don't see a Canadian person in the interior mindscape of the poet, we see an Indian person ruminating over beliefs, customs, ideals and values that *were* his but *are* now on the verge of collapse in the country of his adoption.

With the blurring of boundaries in the mental landscape that once surrounded his entire being, Gill is subjected to a nomadic subjectivity, concerning his status in the new land. In this new setting, he is constantly territorialised, deterritorialised and reterritorialised, creating a gaping void of uncertainty that makes him nostalgic for his mother's warmth:

> I wish to breathe undisturbed
> within the walls of my womb (*DOP*, 48)

As Parthasarathy suggests, "exile," self-imposed or otherwise, makes one learn that "roots are deep."[6] Stephen Gill is an illustration of the truth of this statement. It is perhaps his migration to Canada that explains his persistent obession with the Indian past, both familial and racial, and it is this obsession that constitutes a major theme in all his poetry and is potently expressed:

> A root unprotected
> I need a wind
> loving and kind. (*FOT*, 96)

His memories of the moon beams of his homeland, absorbed through the eyes of a sensitive and observant boy, create an immediate need of warmth in the dismal land he is inhabiting:

> Move not away moon!
> your beams I need
> for the dismal land. (*FOT*, 94)

Gill's nostalgia for his homeland is not solely romantic, it is rather based on the harsh realities of life as everyday life in this new land has its own measure of mystery and dread. His poems reflect an ironic consciousness for the generality of human loss and pain, a sense of disenchantment with the spurious commercial prosperity and a feeling of despondency at the world-crisis the society is heading towards.

Gill has taken to writing furiously as his integrity as a humanitarian is challenged with insulting frequency everytime he encounters waste, loss and mutual destruction. He stridently denounces forces that promote extreme and vicious nationalism or fundamentalism. He liberates his mind through his poems and reveals his socio-political concerns by exposing human animus and jealousy that heighten existential agonies of modern life:

> The land of devils is empty
> because its occupants
> extend desert of savagery[7]

Gill delineates a basic struggle of the soul, the mind and the body to comprehend life in its totality: what he communicates through the poetic medium is a confrontation of his whole being with reality and his response to it in a pungent and straightforward manner. The overall atmosphere created in the poems reflecting his socio-political awareness is one of gloom and despair with a degree of pronounced melancholia. Disappointment is the keynote of this melancholy whether with edgy complications of social insecurity or with insoluble problems of political instability. The poet tries to achieve his goal to instil a sense of mortal fear in his reader and extends his sense of desperation into sensitive and sympathetic minds with the help of using strong words and phrases in arresting alliteration and assonance. The expressions like 'murky marshes,' 'ruthless locusts,' 'fetters . . . cranking,' 'vomit violence,' 'ghost of sorrows,' 'gloom of violence,' 'dust of despicable horror,' 'self-surrounding cells of egoism,' 'spiteful robots,' 'suffocative islands' etc. reveal a picture of devitalised society in the ensuing darkness of which the poet is jaded and lost.

He notices an unquenchable thirst for the manna whose source seems to have dried up suddenly because noxious germs of anarchy are let loose on the socio-political stratosphere: a sense of uneasiness about our hastening confusedly towards unknown ends is all the poet can make out of the modern society.

Gill, therefore, finds nothing to rejoice, for example, on the eve of New Year, which overwhelms him with a mood of gloom; he finds this day same as the days of the previous week or "even last year".

The wilful ghosts of sorrow
have not dissolved
nor have the fogs of ignorance
which float over the cold tombs.[8]

The poet goes on to observe ironically: "If nights were replaced by days/just by thinking/the corners of darkness/would have been lit by now./Eater of stale crumbs/in the mornings/should have been welcomed/by the appetizing smells/of fresh and warm foods./The hours of suffering/would have been reduced,/joys lasted longer/and lives changed." The poem, like a prism, reflects the unchanging social scene which is gnawed by hunger, death, sorrow and suffering, as ever, and "life" does not "wear another mantle;/only calendars become new."

With the use of classical/religious allusion of fallen angels, in the poem "Beelzebub of Demands," Gill cleverly mocks at the "seductive moans of social deities." Continuance of moral laxities, indulgence in sensuality, and political corruption and exploitation strike a staggering blow to the entire social system and the poet experiences an intense need to break the strings:

But how can I do it
when the Beelzebub of demands
chop off my wings.[9]

He goes on to say that channels of electronic media entertainment have added to isolation of individuals and people have increasingly become insensitive to simple pleasure like chatting over a cup of tea or caring and sharing:

I wish to sit down
to talk and talk

and talk more
about this and that
over cups of tea.
But how and with whom
when all are hooked
to their own TVs.

Socio-political upheavals causing loss of human values make Stephen Gill acutely conscious of the spiritual barrenness of the time. Gross human apathy towards the suffering of fellow-beings makes the poet question both the forces of racism and humanism:

Which humanity do you talk about?
I saw her grisly dance
yesterday
at the railway station
where a handful of hooligans
scorned and hit a youth
of a different shade.
A wave of people rushed by,
either to catch a train
or to go home.[10]

Gill is more than pained to see that "No soul had the time/or maybe the courage,/ to let those fallen angels know/they have derided the Creator."

Gill's political poems reveal his anger at the foul play and sinister game of senseless vendetta played by "discriminators" who crown humanity with thorns and hang it on the cross of dreams. These "traders of dead bodies" squeeze the last vestige of blood from life and "in the grave of aspirations" of helpless man "reptiles" find their "home." He sadly observes that "paucity of bridges" between the "islands of tensions" thickens the "darkness of doubts."

"Who would stop/the ravages of global village/by the fury of the explosives?" (*DOP*, 49) is Gill's ironic question to his conscience. Anxieties related to war, terrorism, human rights violation, religious radicalism, hunger, racial discrimination, ecological imbalances etc. are some of the major issues that sit heavy on his conscience:

> I asked my consicence
> if it had perceived
> in the eyes of humankind
> the unshed tears
> of hurts and humiliations.
> A touch of scorn in its silence
> nettled me to ask
> if it had ever heard
> the bricks of my cries
> falling on the blades of the environment.[11]

An overpowering panic in the poet's psyche caused due to war ravages seems to be the extension of his socio-political concerns.

The humanity has witnessed the naked dance of death in the form of world wars and the worst spectacle of it was displayed in the use of atomic weapon during the second world war. The poet is aware of savagery across the globe: "Humans look for an Oasis/in human blood." (*DS*, 47) However, the taste of blood was not enough for 'warmongers' and the Iraq-Iran war and Gulf war sponsored by America left the mute spectators of the whole world aghast at the large scale destruction caused by sophisticated techniques of massacre. Gill's sensitivity is aroused at these instances of ruthless cult of man.

The poet, a firm believer in democracy, decries war which disintegrates society and tears apart a country with all-round devastation: "carnages waged,/the delights of countless wives/ subdued;/numerous men/lost their sight;/and many more maimed./Lofty dreams crushed./Laps of mothers are empty now./ . . . Our homes now better adorned/with the thorns of hatred;/ . . . man is to breathe his last/in the smoke." (*DOP*, 13-14) War is self-defeating, it is fraud, declares Gill, and wonders "what is today's man." He can't understand the puzzle, the contraditions—love for animals but hatred for humanity—perpetrated by man of today. (*DOP*, 23) He pleads for love, harmony and peace, and knows "Peace cannot swim/on the blood waves/ for a happier future/let us build bridges now," (*DOP*, 23) killing the serpent within "that vomits lava of hostility." (*DOP*, 37)

Poem after poem, Gill points to the continually deepening tribulations of people everywhere—contentions and disputes, mutual deceits, sudden calamities, misery and distress, convulsions of war, spread of inveterate diseases, hunger and poverty, religious fundamentalism and fanaticism—that have upset the world's equilibrium. To add to this, scientific advancement has made human beings "a prisoner of chaotic nights." Increasing withdrawal from the world of peaceful co-existence has inflamed a self-loving, short-sighted tendency in them, creating a world where the only certainty is that nothing is certain:

> the urchins of stinking strife—
> and dusty pride in the march
> of technology and science. (*DOP*, 48)

> Science would write
> the last chapter
> and religious bigotry
> shall provide the title
> to the last dance on the hills
> inhabited by the children
> of racial insanity.
> The clouds shall rage
> to bear witness.[12]

Upset over "pollution, panic, and poisonous civic life" and prospects of a third world war, the poet seeks refuge in his own "calming womb/beyond the embraces of robots/and bursts of inhuman cries" (*DOP*, 48) that make the dove of peace wild. He pities people who are proud of fiddling "with noxious gases/and of raining/virus and fire/to deface our mother-earth" but who are not proud "of a single aircraft/accident-free/to ensure our travels/carefree." (*DOP*, 15)

Gill looks for poet-philosophers whose voice is "mightier than cannons" just as the promoter of universal brotherhood condemns the "fanatic mind" which is born of ignorance and is "death's cradle." (*DOP*, 50) In his disappointment, Gill, the seeker of world's welfare, supplicates to God: "Give us wisdom/not to uproot our orchard./The earth./Thy footstool,/enlivens all/O Lord. . . . /Give us now/a gown of humility/to wear/water of tranquillity/to drink/O Father." (*DOP*, 52-53)

The seeker in him considers war, for whatever reasons—political, economic, racial, ethnic, religious—a derision to the Creator, who cares for everyone and reveals the secret of undisturbed peace. Since "the workship of violence . . . leads to the temple of hatred," he urges people and governments not to rest on their political power, economic strength or armies but follow the path of justice and promote the highest interests of the whole of humanity.

Gill turns to poetry to search for unity in the multiplicity of cultural norms. He tries to assimilate cultural diversity to explore himself and discover his own creative tissues:

> The womb of life
> fabric of civilizations
> author of prosperities
> mirror of wisdom
> sonata of peace. (*SFH*, 27)

For him genuine poetry is an antidote to suffering, which he can transform "into nutrients" with divine grace. As he prays: "Display in them/Your will;/fuse them with your beauty." (*SFH*, 9) The poet has a strong faith in poetry:

> I wish my poetry to be friendly
> to pacify the tiger of violence
> and to assemble flowers of all hues
> into a single bouquet. (*SFH*, 12)

As a potent voice of humanity he warns his readers about the looming disaster to befall mankind if the present generation does not take concrete measures to maintain world peace and harmony:

> Humans have to change
> demons to go, and
> rusted fetters to break
> before the glory of harmony
> stretches soothing wings
> over the decaying orchards, and
> the smile of its presence
> disperses the clouds of gloom
> to free the rays of beauty. (*SFH*, 27)

The poet looks for the ambrosia that can instill corpuscles of love and tolerance into the masses whose leadership indulges in internecine struggle. His poetic cult is the cult of humanity which reverberates with universal love, manifesting itself in the form of devotion through self-abandoning supplication, through love for nature, through love for the beloved, and through commitment for peace and harmony.

Gill's poetry is, in fact, an epitome of philosophy as much based in the Hindu metaphysics as it is founded on Christian faith. The poems echo oriental philosophy in that they make the readers turn inward in search of the meaning of existence. It's only through knowing one's own self one can understand the outer world and the society at large:

> It was on the crossroad of desires
> where I met Me.
> Looking into my eyes,
> he shook my hand at that cold moment
> and then dissolved slowly
> like evening
> in a crowd of strange faces.

In his silent sight
I perceived a glow
despair
and the joy of flying birds.

Under the brow of cloudy skies
those deep eyes
dropped the dew of innocence
on the wings of my guilt
which I carry still
while searching for Me. ("A Handshake")

Christianity propagates love for mankind through broadening one's outlook and realising the presence of God in one's being. In search of love one need not look outside because it lies in abundance hidden in one's own self. Only the presence of this divine love should be realised through cultivating a harmonious feeling for fellow beings. When it is achieved, presence of God will be felt among the mortals:

I live in your veins
your blood is my abode
I am the love, search your heart. (*FOT*, 16)

Sometimes Gill's poems sound like the sacred utterances of a devotee madly in love with his goddess and carries the essence of the tradition of Mirabai and Jaidev: "Your smiles emitted might/the blue eyes gave sign/I called you shrine." (*FOT*, 38)

His love for the beloved and Nature (*Prakriti*) often swap places with the elements of nature and, whenever in dismay, he longs to see her face which is the melody of his life:

A melody
that I die to hear
from my window of dismay
when down goes the sun
is your face. (*FOT*, 48)

For him the moon, dew, flame, rain, rainbow, etc. are the life-giving sources, the blessed and positive aspects of life that carry cells of love in their veins, i.e. the "elysian charm" or "God's wonder." He wants to submit himself to this eternal source of joy. In fact he wants his love to culminate in joy. Even in the face of unhappiness, cruelty and disillusionment, the poet in Gill wants to be rejuvenated by the grace of love, which he seeks "not in dreams/and the thoughts in solitude" but "along the serene self-composed clouds." (*FOT*, 56-57) Some of his poems smack of several classical Indian poets who metaphorically compared their lady-love with the 'mountains,' 'buds,' 'seas' and 'sun's rays,' or as distraught lovers bemoaned:

> Abandoning all,
> I longed to kiss
> your lips;
> frozen indifferent
> they kept me afar. (*FOT*, 24)

Stephen Gill seeks to realise his love in "a sinking star of the morning" even as his lady love might not bear the "majesty of oceans" or "the secret of fragrance," or "the pride of youth" or "the beauty of the moon." Aware of the fleeting nature of time as he is, Gill faces the reality of life and death, hope and dismay, gain and loss with a sense of equanimity: "Under the ashes of the last night/half-dead embers glow again/while thieving time passes by." (*FOT*, 23)

The poet dreams a life that, against all odds and limitations, shall give him all he desires. The "Elysian gleams" or the "Elysian charm" he looks for in his experiences are in fact indicative of an attitude, which is positive, constructive, and humane, with an understanding of the discordant reality of life, especially greed, hunger, pollution, and war. He seeks to live in the "dignity of hills/vision of heaven" (*FOT*, 62) to counter his aloneness. (*FOT*, 35) As he romantically imagines:

> I shall build a cabin there

with the stuff simple
sleep there as I wish
awake to music serene
attuned one with nature.
I shall hibernate somewhere
in a lonely, unvisited spot
amidst the Elysian bounties
embracing peace surpassing all. (*DOP*, 44-45)

The idealist in Gill expresses a longing for the elysium fields that could be free from social, political, territorial, moral, ethnic, and ecological pollution. He dreams of a world where people would harmoniously co-exist forgetting petty discrimination on the basis of caste, race, colour or nationality and would love each other accepting individual differences. This love would metamorphose man by healing and bestowing upon man the power to heal; making a healer of a man.

Gill's poetry testifies to his inner need to live more deeply with greater awareness, to know other's experience and to know his own experience well. He recreates situations and experiences that are significant and focused for his readers to participate and derive a better understanding of the contemporary world. He broadens and deepens their experience, using language as an instrument of persuasion and as an aid to living in a world which excels in self-destruction. His purpose is to arouse and awake, to shock one into life, to make one more alert and responsive to the happenings around, to make one more alive.

Stephen Gill is a poet of values—universal peace and love, oneness and wholeness of human race, respect for human right, and a social structure designed to produce and promote justice. The poet, who considers his poems a part of his spiritual self, urges abolition of racial, religious, political and economic prejudices and seeks equal opportunities and privileges for men and women, adoption of a world code of human rights and responsibilities, and creation of a world federal government to heal the dissensions that divide people. He knows religious fanaticism and hatred are a world-devouring fire whose violence none can quench. God alone can deliver humanity from this desolating affliction. His principal concern is to rescue the ignorant or fallen from the slough of impending extinction. Features like the postmodernist self-understanding, sense of doubt, despair, uncertainty, futility, rejection of European/American dominance and assertion of individuality are some of the hallmarks of his creativity.

As an ethnic writer and poet, he enriches the 'mosaic-tapestry' of Canadian culture and values with his Indian background and Eastern learning. The "immigrant" sensibility of the novelist Gill extends into the poet Gill, whose creative negotiation absorbs conflict of cultures without being bitter. A crusading idealism overwhelms him with emotions of love and tolerance just as his missionary zeal is a reflection of the utopian state he fervently desires to achieve through aesthetic endeavours. He strives to make "society more rational and more friendly" to promote brotherhood; he loves the world and dedicates himself to the service of the entire human race.

NOTES

1. Stephen Gill, *The Flowers of Thirst (FOT)* (Ontario: Vesta Publication, 1990).
2. Stephen Gill, "Blind and Deaf," *Gypsy*, 17, 1991, p. 62.
3. Stephen, Gill, "A New Canadian in Toronto," *Star India*, July 9, 1993, p. 15.
4. Stephen Gill, *The Dove of Peace* (*DOP*) (2nd Ed., New York: M.A.F. Press, 1993), p. 27.
5. Stephen Gill, *Songs for Harmony* (*SFH*) (New Jersey: Rose Shell Press, 1993).
6. R. Parthasarathy, *Rough Passage* (Delhi: Oxford University Press, 1977), p. 17.
7. Stephen Gill, *Divergent Shades* (*DS*) (Ranchi: Writers' Forum, 1995), p. 47.
8. Stephen Gill, "On the New Year," *Seaway News*, December 26, 1994, p. 2.

9. Stephen Gill, "Beelzebub of Demands," *From Both Sides of the Ocean*, January-February 1995, p. 23.
10. Stephen Gill, "To Humanists," *al-mohajer*, Issue No. 2-3, Febuary-March 1994.
11. Stephen Gill, "A Conversation," *Conscience Canada*, No. 60, Winter 1994.
12. Stephen Gill, "Last Dance," *Twilight Ending*, vol. 2, No. 2, May 1996, p. 21.

Critical Response to Rushdie

C.N. RAMACHANDRAN

Before I begin my paper, I have to make two clarifications: (1) strictly speaking, my paper is not about Rushdie as such: it is about the nature of critical discourses in general, and in India, in particular, taking Rushdie as an illustrative case. (2) The theoretical framework of the paper, which I assume and do not lay out in detail, is the discourse theory of Michel Foucault; and, in particular, his argument that at any given point of time, it is the dominant discourse prevailing in a particular field that determines what is knowledge and what is not.

There are two parts in my paper: while the first analyses the major trends of critical responses to Rushdie's works, the second discusses the implications as well as consequences of such critical responses.

I

To describe the critical attention and approval accorded to Rushdie as a novelist, today, is to belabour the obvious. Hence, I shall be very brief. Rushdie's second novel, *Midnight's Children*, was published in 1980. Immediately, *The New Yorker* hailed him as a "glittering novelist—one with startling imaginative and intellectual resources," and went on to compare him with Garcia Marquez. In 1981, the novel was given the prestigious Booker McConnell Award, followed by James Tait Black Memorial Prize, and the English-speaking Union Literary Award. To crown it all, after a decade, the Booker-of-Booker Award was bestowed upon it.

After the publication of *Midnight's Children*, within no time the British and American critics as well as the Media appropriated him to the bandwagon of postmodernism and postcolonialism. Steven Connor, for instance, brackets Rushdie with Borges and Beckett in his influential book, *Postmodernist Culture* (1989), and says: "Self-conscious, de-centered, sceptical, and playfully polymorphous, the postmodernist literary text from Borges to Beckett to Rushdie is an ideal object of analysis."[1] James Harrison, in his book on Rushdie in the Twayne series, approves of the "magic realism" in *Midnight's Children*, discusses in detail the postcolonial and meta-fictional features of the novel, and moves to this grand conclusion: "To say that language and meaning crumble, disintegrate, deconstruct themselves only endlessly and phoenix like to reconstruct themselves, is merely to say that they partake of and reflect the human condition."[2] Amin Malak finds *The Satanic Verses* a daring and ambitious "historiographical metafiction," "deploying various tropes and encompassing multiple layers of signification, while operating within a postmodernist, counter-culture context."[3]

Indian critics weren't, and aren't far behind in their tributes to Rushdie. Not very surprisingly, in this context, *The New Indian Novel in English*, edited by Viney Kripal in 1990, has five essays on Rushdie.[4] There have been quite a few doctoral and M.Phil. dissertations on Rushdie in Indian universities. However, for the sake of brevity, Makarand Paranjape's article, "Inside and Outside the Whale" can be considered a representative Indian evaluation of Rushdie, barring a few exceptions. Paranjape sums up his views on Rushdie in these words: "This momentous book (i.e. *Midnight's Children)* really jolted the very foundation of the Indian-English novel. Its energy, its self-indulgence, irresponsibility, disorder, and cockiness really shocked the daylights out of the staid form of the Indian-English novel. . . . To put it simply—so long the Indian-English novel lived inside the whale before this big book. . . . Realism, consistent characters, linearity, order are out; non-linearity, fantasy, and disorder are in. . . . I can name heaps of novels which bear an influence of Rushdie's liberating touch."[5] That after all this panegyric, in the very next paragraph, Paranjape finds that "the author is a hoax" is curious if nothing else.

On the whole, the critical consensus, both Indian and Anglo-American, seems to be that (a) Rushdie's mode of narration is magic realism, (b) he is postcolonial and postmodernist, and (c) his use of English is "innovative" and "decolonizing." Let us consider these a bit more closely.

(a) Magic Realism has been variously defined as an attempt to transcend the limitation of Realism, a free mixture of fantasy and reality, a mode that holds the mirror "at a slight angle to reality." It is viewed as denying "the hegemony of bourgeois Realism" by Arun Mukherjee;[6] as a "micro-macro synthesis" by T.N. Dhar.[7] However, what is interesting to note is that it was Rushdie himself who first claimed for his fiction the mode of Magic Realism; and immediately critics hurriedly endorsed the claim.

What happens to Magic Realism when it is used as an instrument of ambitious political and religious allegory? Consider Mahound and "Return to Jahilia" chapters in *The Satanic Verses*, which show Mahound as a calculating businessman, one who is ready to make compromises, and who finally marries twelve denizens of a brothel. If any reader, Muslim or non-Muslim, feels offended, Rushdie can always claim that it is a dream-sequence, that it is the dream of a popular Hindi film-star, and that at that point the dreamer is drunk. Such an argument forecloses any meaningful discussion and debate. If this instance appears to be an extreme case, consider these from *Midnight's Children*. Who uses such expressions as "urine-drinking Finance Minister," "The Widow," and "labia-lipped man"? Not the author, but the narrator—the crazy, impotent, and constantly up-rooted Saleem Sinai. In other words, magic realism in Rushdie can also be viewed as a technique of *escape*—escape from any responsibility, ideological as well as ethical.

(b) As noted earlier, Rushdie is considered a pre-eminent postcolonial writer because, according to Steve Connor, "Such texts expose the fictionality of history itself,"[8] because, according to Dieter Riemenschneider, "in its absurdity, (the absurd of

Rushdie) exposes the extent of the historian's and historiographer's hubris."[9] On the theoretical plane, all these views are unimpeachable. But, let us see them in practice.

Early in the novel, *Midnight's Children*, the narrator talks about his grandfather getting caught in the Jallianwala Bagh massacre. The narrator describes the crowd, and then says: "The fifty-one men enter the compound and take positions. . . . As Brigadier Dyer issues a command the sneeze hits my grandfather full in the face. Yaaakh-thooo he sneezes and falls forward, losing his balance, following his nose and thereby saving his life."[10] I am sure, even an ideal historian wouldn't be so objective as to treat the massacre and an old man's nose with equal seriousness.

Or, consider the description of the linguistic re-organization of India, in 1967. According to the narrator, the boundaries of the new states were "walls of words." The movement for a Marathi-state and its clashes with the Gujarati agitation—all these are "old dead struggles between the barren angularity of Marathi . . . and Gujarati's boggy Kathiawari softness." (226) Clearly, the narrator here is one who has no idea of languages, and the symbiotic relationship between a language, its speakers and their culture. No wonder, then, a little later, he records that an innocent rhyme in Gujarati sparked off a riot in which many people were killed. To be aware of Gujarati domination in the industrial Bombay, to be aware of the economic deprivation of the Maharashtrians in Maharashtra—to be aware of all these complicated issues would be to really historicize the language-riots of the Fifties. But, for a man like Rushdie, who is supposed to subvert history, these riots take place because Indians aren't rational creatures.

That brings us to a more important aspect of Rushdie's historiography. As is obvious, in *Midnight's Children*, Rushdie attempts to chronicle simultaneously the histories of an individual and a nation. What is the nature of the national history that emerges from *Midnight's Children*? The overall picture of post-independence India that Rushdie documents in the novel is one of immature and emotional people and a leaderless country.

Here, people start killing one another on any pretext; they are all hypocrites; and European ideas and ideals are borrowed only to be mocked at in this country. "India, the new myth—a collective fiction in which anything was possible, a fable rivalled only by the two other mighty fantasies: money and God." (130) How is this historiography (if such a term can be used), one wonders, different from the colonial histories of James Mill and others? As Sara Suleri, an eminent postcolonial critic, comments wryly, "its reinvention of history is thus shamefully fraught with the fear that finally, postcolonial narrative *can only replicate* the will to power that impelled colonial historical texts."[11]

Finally, coming to Rushdie's use of English, it is supposed to be "born out of a creative consciousness," and "a subversion of English language."[12] But what one actually finds in him is a gratuitous mix of English, Hindi, and Urdu words, resulting in what he himself calls "Chutnification of English." In fact, on more than one occasion, such diction comforts the Western audience of Rushdie that after all Indians—or Asians in general—can only use a sort of Pidgin English, or what used to be called Butler English. Creative use of English one finds in Raja Rao, in Amitav Ghosh, not in Rushdie.

II

At this point, justifiably, one may intervene to wonder why I am making such a fuss of Rushdie being a bad writer. If one doesn't like him, one could ignore him? However, once we move beyond our likes and dislikes of Rushdie (and such others) and reflect on the factors that have established him as a pre-eminent Indian writer in English (after all, bagging a Booker-of-Booker award isn't a joke) the issues that I am interested in do not seem to be that simple.

To start with, the Rushdie-phenomenon clearly establishes the fact that today writers are made or marred by mass media and institutions, national and international. Once such institutions as the Booker, the Pulitzer, etc. create the reputation of a writer, the media take over; and, through their organized tours, personal interviews, talk-shows, and seminars systematically legitimize that reputation, giving a stamp of authority. Once a writer is legitimized, he/she forms the core subject of University-syllabi and research. In such a situation, very few—especially in the Third World—have the temerity to question the legitimization.

And, who are the writers and which are the works that are so legitimized by the Anglo-American institutions?—Writers like Rushdie and before him, Vikram Seth, Naipaul, Arun Kolatkar, and such others. That is, those writers who gladly take on the mantle of "privileged native informations," to use Gayatri Spivak's cutting phrase.[13] They assure their Western audience that their system, their structure, and their ideology are the only sane alternative for the entire world. In other words, the Anglo-American institutions including the media, more often consciously, continue the centuries-old imperialist view of the Orient as the Other, even after the collapse of all the empires.

The fact that Rushdie and his ilk are more easily legitimized than others by the powerful Western institutions, guaranteeing them fabulous wealth as well as fame, lures younger writers in the Third World to follow in their footsteps. Even a cursory glance at the new Indian writers in English amply proves this point. Upamanyu Chatterjee's *English, August* has as its protagonist, an IAS officer, who can only indulge in masturbation during his official tours. The Novel begins thus: "Amazing mix, the English we speak. Hazaar fucked Urdu and American. . . . A thousand fucked, really fucked." *The Revised Kamasutra* by Richard Crasta (which has an imposing subtitle, A novel of Colonization and Desire) also has an IAS officer cum potential writer as its protagonist, who, at the end of the novel, fantasizes a glorious blow-job by his New York agent. It is also full of expletives, Konkani words, and so-called Indian English.[15]

Namita Gokale's *Paro* is, according to *Evening Standard*, "unexpected for its erotic content, frank language and sly humour."[16] The list can go on and on. And, significantly, almost all such novels have been published abroad.

Another natural corollary of such Western selective legitimization of Third-World writers is that other writers tend to be ignored and sidelined in their own countries. On the occasion of the 50th year of Indian independence, it is Rushdie and not Raja Rao or Shashi Deshpande that gets invited by the *New York Times* to write about India and Indian literature. That Rushdie, in his article, made the preposterous claim that creative writing in India was only in English and not in any regional languages was only expected, reassuring the British and American readers that after all colonization was not such a bad thing to happen to India. The institutionalized stature of a writer like Rushdie grows so imposing that the Foreword to a published doctoral dissertation on Rushdie has this audacious statement: "[Rushdie has shown] that Indian writer in English does not have to write idiomatic and grammatically correct English like R.K. Narayan."[17] Madhusudan Rao, the author of the book, has this to say on Rushdie's use of English: "To this extent, perhaps, Rushdie achieves a greater degree of success than the other Indian writers in English, particularly Raja Rao, R.K. Narayan and Mulk Raj Anand." (165) It is this aspect of the Rushdie phenomenon—a sort of literary Darwinism—that one finds so alarming.

Most importantly, the Indian response to the Rushdie-phenomenon (with a few exceptions) documents that we still accept Anglo-American evaluations at their face-value; and it is this aspect that is most disturbing.

For instance, most Indian critics (Makarand Paranjape, Arun P. Mukherjee, etc.) wax eloquent about how Rushdie's novels expose "bourgeois Liberalism," ignoring the fact that ideologies in different societies serve different purposes. It is true that in nineteenth century England and America, liberal Humanism, with its strong emphasis on individuality, was cultivated to serve vested interests of the upper classes. But it is also true that the same ideology, accepted by Raja Rammohun Roy, Gokhale, Nehru, and others, gave much needed impetus to the caste-tradition-ridden Indian society toward modernisation, giving, for the first time in its long history, a recognition as well as a social position to the Tribals, the lower castes, and—most importantly—women. Even today, it is the same "bourgeois Liberalism that is needed to keep this pluralistic Indian society intact.

In fact, one thought, it was obvious that ideologies and concepts change their nature and function when they move from one society to another. For instance, Modernism to Eliot and Joyce (and their society) meant submission of the individual to Tradition. But it meant in India, with its rigid and hoary traditions, the liberation of the individual from the tyranny of religious, social, and literary traditions. Similarly, the much-bandied term Realism. Rushdie and his kind are credited with "breaking out of Realism" and rejecting "the hegemony of bourgeois Realism."[18] What is "bourgeois Realism"? The Realism one finds in Dickens and Galsworthy turns out to be something different in the Indian context. Commenting on Mahasweta Devi's "Standayini," brilliantly translated by herself as "Breast-Giver," Gayatri Spivak makes the following pointed comment: "'Much third world fiction is still caught in realism' (whereas the international literatures of the First World have graduated into language games) is a predictable generalization. This is often the result of a lack of acquaintance with the language of the original. . . . Speaking in code, then, we might say that to diagnose all third World literature in English translation, by way of sanctioned ignorance of the original, as a realism not yet graduated into language-games is a species of stress upon the wood-apple-type-herbal remedies correspondingly." (267-68)

Rushdie, perhaps, was not aware of the full significance of his words when he pontificated in a PEN conference: "But the effects of the empire linger on. Those who were made powerful then remain, for the most part, powerful now."[19] How true! How very true!!

NOTES

1. Steve Connor, *Postmodernist Culture: An Introduction to Theories of the Contemporary* (New York: Basil Blackwell, 1989), p. 128.
2. Amin Malak, "Reading The Crisis: The Polemics of Salman Rushdie's *The Satanic Verses*," *A Review of International English Lit-*

erature, 20:4 (Oct. 1989), p.176.

3. Viney Kirpal, ed., *The New Indian Novel in English: A Study of the 1980s* (New Delhi: Allied, 1990).
4. James Harrison, *Salman Rushdie* (New York: Twayne, 1992), pp. 10, 67-68.
5. Makarand Paranjape, "Inside and Outside the Whale: Politics and the New Indian English Novel," in Viney Kirpal, p. 220.
6. Arun P. Mukherjee, "Characterization in Salman Rushdie's *Midnight's Children*: Breaking Out of Realism and Seeking the Alienation Effect," in Viney Kirpal, p. 113.
7. A.N. Dhar, "Micro-Macro Symbiosis: The Form of Salman Rushdie's *Midnight's Children*," *Journal of Indian Writing in English*, (Jan. 1985), 22.
8. Steve Connor, pp. 126-27. Here he is commenting upon Linda Hutcheon's view of postmodernist literature as "historiographic metafiction."
9. Dieter Riemenschneider, "History and the Individual in Anita Desai's *Clear Light of Day* and Salman Rushdie's *Midnight's Children*," in Viney Kirpal, p. 196.
10. Salman Rushdie, *Midnight's Children* (1980, New York: Avon Books, 1982), p. 35.
11. Sara Suleri, *The Rhetoric of English India* (Chicago: University of Chicago Press, 1992), p. 176. She relates this condition to a "schizophrenic anticipation of audience . . . built into the text" such as *Shame* and *Midnight's Children*.
12. Madhusudan Rao, *Salman Rushdie's Fiction: A Study* (New Delhi: Sterling, 1992), pp. 165, 167. In fact, the banality of such books is evidenced when, after just two pages, the author claims that "in Rushdie, what appeals most . . . is his use of chaste British idiom." p. 168.
13. Gayatri Chakravarti Spivak, *In Other Worlds: Essays in Cultural Politics* (New York: Methuen, 1987), p. 256.
14. Upamanyu Chatterjee, *English, August* (New Delhi: Rupa, 1989).
15. Richard Crasta, *The Revised Kamasutra* (New Delhi: Penguin, 1993).
16. As quoted by Devinder Mohan, in Viney Kirpal, p. 136.
17. V. Rangan, Foreword to Madhusudan Rao, p. viii.
18. Arun P. Mukherjee, title of the essay, and p. 113.
19. As quoted by Arun P. Mukherjee, p. 112.

Rushdie's Politics of Understatement: The Subaltern and History of *Shame*

SEEMA BHADURI

Rushdie's *Shame*[1] reconstructs the sordid political history of Pakistan bringing to light the deep socio-cultural imbalances that have shaped this history. Rushdie uses the technique of magic realism to situate the publically acknowledged facts of this history—the coups, murders and rigged elections in the context of the not so publically known grim atmosphere of fear, intrigue, humiliation and desperate defiance that govern the lives and minds of the people of Pak.

In order to highlight the monstorsity of their behaviour, Rushdie likens his characters to hideous creatures of Greek mythology—centaurs, werewolves, wraiths (pp. 30, 40). His heroine is a cannibal. One finds a strong resemblance between this type of presentation and the general image of Asia and Africa as they appear in the European and American press.[2] Here is a language that barely conceals the horror and contempt of the 'superior' white races for the dark, semi-civilized continents of Asia and Africa.[3]

This paper seeks to establish that the characters of the novel are in their deeds, moved by historical forces much larger than their powers of understanding. In his treatment of the characters Rushdie does not address all the forces squarely. He glosses over much of history perhaps for the purpose of convenience.

Rushdie hinges his narrative upon a grim paradox—one of the prime anomalies that dog these people: the mutually hostile medieval and modernist ages coexist in the life and minds of the people of Pak. The independent Republic of Pakistan claims to be of the twentieth century—the age of science and secularism, of individualism and political independence, the age of nationalism as well as globalization—in short the era of westernization. But the native mind and thought is medieval. So one finds religious fundamentalism and retrogressive sexual ethics imposed in the domestic sphere, that is, the sphere of the women, and the pursuit of libertinism and modernist principles of republicanism remains the perspective of the English-speaking young men.

In his analysis of the nature of the gruesome violence that seizes Pak intermittently, Rushdie clarifies that it is universal to human nature. It arises from the dual feelings of helplessness and rage that seize man after prolonged periods of humiliation and defeat. The French people before the Revolution and many Asians of today have exhibited the traits most strongly. Yet the political drama of Pak strongly appears to have been parodied with chiefly the Westernized audience in mind and from the high point of Western standards of civilization. A close reading of the text itself however highlights legacies of colonial history that make the West at once equally responsible for the sordid drama.

While the episodes in the novel do reveal the erosion of justice and the bloody betrayal of humanitarian principles, the narrative offers also an alternate, cogent and consistent reading as the natural denouement of the colonial enterprise. Fundamental anomalies have crept into Pak's body politic in the very process of its formation. In the absence of any higher cultural consciousness or spiritual legacy—the kind that was available to India and by reflection, to the characters of *Midnight's Children*—the Pakistani subaltern will indeed turn grotesque in living out these legacies. This is not to exonerate them of their crimes, but merely to put these into perspective.

Nationalism is a European legacy perpetuated in the erstwhile colonies largely by Euro-educated natives. It was basically a socio-political expedient, a pact made among people sharing the same language and culture for maximum trade-profit. It must be remembered too that it led first to colonization and then, to the world-wars.[4] For the politicians in the postcolonial nations—

it serves exactly as it does its parent-nations—a means of trading for maximum profit, but, in both cases, dished out wrapped in the pious rhetoric of freedom and development. The native politicians are doing among their own people what the Europeans did in their colonies—plunder, and where necessary, bloodshed. One therefore feels that to flesh out this very story for those very western/westernized minds is not merely ironic—it is cruel.

As *Shame* illustrates, the history of Pakistan records a chain of betrayals, wars and coups which have their roots in the medieval time-frame. Centuries of slavery and oppression have frozen the spirit to action. In consequence, death and disease, knavery and debauchery make the only events of their history. (76) This shows the absence of any vital cultural, martial or spiritual tradition, that, coming down from the past, could have directed the people in the present towards some envisioned future. In such a state of affairs, sudden political freedom came perhaps as a dubious gift, the subaltern now finding it necessary to exercise his 'free' will in a world that is both modern and medieval and therefore, neither.

Set on these lines, *Shame* becomes a grim, black comedy, operating at two levels. Here erstwhile slaves like Iskander Harappa shadow-mime the colonisers's high-handed despotism upon their own people. At the same time, *Shame* is a grotesque drama of a medieval jingo of nationalism, secularism, mass-elections etc. But what makes this drama comic at yet another level is the twentieth century European eye and voice of censure lodged in the writer-narrator. He stands, as he claims, at an angle to the reality of Pak, but that angle is in no way 'slight.' (29) It may be pertinent here to recall that this voice has itself evolved after more than four centuries of violent, vicissitude-ridden debate on intellectual positions in politics and philosophy and is very largely consonant with its indigenous intellectual and cultural moorings.

Iskander Harappa the licentious dandy-turned President who tries to Westernise the country in no time and the Maulana Dawood-led President Raza Hyder who reads Namaz over the TV five times a day as a compulsory official activity, embody the two facets of the native mind-set, two mutually exclusive socio-temporal spaces. The Pak of Western geo-political mapping—a modernist independent republic with its clubs and ski resorts—jostles with the Pak of burqua-clad women locked away in prison-like mansions and of 'Gatta-marked' divines and Presidents using religion to hold the masses to ransom. This anomaly, a gift of its history, questions the idea of the 'national' identity of Pak.

One of the outcomes of the superimposition of modernism upon minds rooted in ancient systems of belief is the backlash of fundamentalism as is being seen in most parts of Asia and Africa today. As writers like Ashish Nandy have emphasized, religion gives to a people faith, which, perhaps is another word for identity which again in terms of day-to-day living, means moral law, and a sense of direction and of purpose. In this sense, religion brings dignity and encourages creativity. It is not mere ritual, superstitions and black magic. Modernism with its two arms—secularism and materialism—not merely fails to do that, but it outlaws religion as well. The condition of the natives of Pak is the more abject as they are medieval without having the dignity of religion. Their slavery to the English has destroyed their freedom to create and thereby, their faith too. What remains is superstition seen variously in the natives (152) and in Omar's mothers, (132) and ritual seen in President Raza's total subservience to the mullah.

In such an environment, President Iskander's secular hedonism is a premature baby dying with its progenitor. One finds here the ancient truth that freedom is a potential danger to minds and hands that have long been delinked from traditions of creative thought and action. In Karachi and Lahore, it died as Rushdie himself indicates, with the death of the Mughal Empire, with the advent of the English. (33) But thinking and acting go on as a process of nature even when there is no creation. Under the heady influences of freedom, the barbarian impulse turns to destruction and what is there to destroy but the rich relics of the past? So the (anti-) hero destroys the fabulous relics of Persian heritage at the mansion of Nishapur where he was born, and

Iskander's cousin Harappa destroys another set of relics at another ancient mansion in Mohenjo. Rushdie suggests that a recourse to that past could have provided the intellectual Omar an alternative to the sheer libertinism with which his mothers asked him to take on the present. (31, 38) But, like most native intellectuals, he was unprepared to take it. So the only service the priceless antiques could render was to sell for ready money so that their owners are spared the exertion of facing the present!

Omar and Iskander Harappa are neophyte Europeans born of their defeated culture's slavish prostitution to the victorious Western culture.[5] Omar's triune mothers who blatantly invite the British officers to seduce them suggest by the great similarity in all their appearance and behaviour "the operation of some form of communal mind." (19-20) *Shame* is a study of the psyche of a defeated culture. The male ego, thwarted on all sides, finds in women its only material possession that must be protected if she belongs to oneself or robbed if she belongs to another. But Rushdie's women are strong. All the major female characters of *Shame* have one quality in common—the desire to wreck vengeance upon their men and the male-oriented customs that have defined their wretchedness. They do this either through public orgies, or secret liaisons (as Omar's mother do) or by making public their men's shameful deeds through symbols (as do Raza's and Iskander's wives). Sufia apotheosises this process by literally becoming a werewolf, devouring men. This total dissociation between man and woman drives the nail into the very soul of this community. Women are naturally gifted with larger cultural sensibilities and a greater consciousness. It is part of their creative potential. Rushdie therefore makes culture feminine in gender. Deriding culture as womanish, the men forfeit it altogether thereby forfeiting consciousness. And this is at the very root of their decline, for none of the characters has that larger consciousness that could guide vision through and beyond the upheavals of current history and form the shaping spirit of the future. So Rushdie predicts ultimate death and dissolution for his Pak. (286) In the India of *Midnight's Children*, variegated cultural traditions of an almost fathomless past and the rich consciousness that follows has kept alive its ethnic identity. On the other hand the consciousness of the female characters in *Shame* (only they seem to have some) is perforce limited to one of personal suffering and the sense of impending doom. Whatever customs exist are male-oriented. The only honour allowed to women is the awareness of their 'Sharam' which keeps them in burquas and prison-like mansions. Hence the women rebel. Omar's mothers totally refuse to initiate their son into any form of religion or to feel any sense of shame. (38-39) So Omar is appropriately a dissipated rake—a quality inherited at his very conception. But he has something of his paternal culture too. He is very intelligent (36) and like most of the twentieth century European intellectuals he is plagued by fears of the absurdity and the meaninglessness of life. His vertigo, his irrational fears of falling over the edge, his feeling of living in a topsy-turvy world (22) all symbolize this malaise born of loss of faith, in modern Europe. However, as an outsider to that development of Western thought that culminated in this sense of existential angst, Omar finds his condition inexplicable. He lets the annihilating sense of worthlessness lead him to greater dissipation. Omar is the type of the Westernized native, rated very highly by the mother culture for his individuality and intellectuality. They expect him to become a great creator (30) unaware of the spiritual barrenness they have bequeathed to him. He becomes instead, at the behest of his English tutor Rodrigues, a doctor, treating diseases of the mind 'a legitimized voyeur.' (49) How much a nation can do with such intelligentsia is obvious.

Pakistan as seen in *Shame* is faced with a crisis of identity that can express itself only through violence. Its very origin places it in a perpetual two-way strife with its past. While on the one hand it seeks to obliterate its Indian past in order to assert its freedom, this act of obliteration through war and anti-India sentiments links it irretrievably with its past. Hence it is "a peeling, fragmenting palimpsest at war with itself." (87) This anomaly of inheritance Pak cannot but perpetuate in its own history.

The partition has beset Pak with another irremediable problem. Pak comprises of two sets of mutually hostile people—the emigrants from India, and the local populace. While the locals are caught in a fathomless inertia, the Muhajirs (the immigrants) who have left their Indian home, history and culture behind them, begin a scramble for survival at all costs. History (i.e. the Partition) has left them destitute and without identity—"naked and browless." (63) What remains with them now is the mere sense of self and the attendant insecurity which urges them on to seize power by any means—fair or foul. Consequently they are seen taking charge of all affairs of governance and business. But the Partition with all its cataclysmic change has instilled into them a deep fear of all change, hence of all progress and development. Witness Raza Hyder's subservience to the mullah and Bilquis's fear of the Loo—the strong summer winds. Both of them are Mohajirs—both want permanence. Only Sufia who by virtue of being an idiot is pure and can sense the corruption all round, craves for change, but all she can do is to continually rearrange the furniture in the house. (68)

With so many inherent anomalies, perhaps no nation can survive. Rushdie predicts death for his Pak. Death at the hands of the very history that created it—witness the birth of Bangladesh. Besides, having either lost or disowned their culture, the natives have no foundation for their future. Appropriately, Sufia the heroine ends her life after killing her husband the anti-hero. Of course they have no children. Appropriately too, Sufia is born of Mohajirs, and Omar of natives. The split between the two sets is complete.

While Rushdie gives to his readers a very graphic picture of the historical and cultural crisis in Pak, his book has no vital flesh-and-blood character who could have suitably dramatized the enormity of the Western involvement in what has happened and is happening in Pak. The figure of the lone ancient and somewhat eccentric Eduardo Rodrigues, Omar's teacher and foster father, is very pale and suitably distanced image of the white man and his influence on Pak's destiny. Further, Rushdie has made Rodrigues a sterotyped object of ridicule—the like of which we have in our Hindi films—by making his rumoured liaison with the eight-year-old foul-mouthed Farah the topic of much casual gossip. That has further blurred the edges of his identity, making him an absurdly comic, and at the same time, harmless figure.

Rushdie is a novelist in whose works historiography comes with the force of authenticity and directness of appeal because he has fused the conventional distance between writer, narrator and reader, on the one hand and the narrative and the reader on the other, not only by suing the narrative devices of the oral story-teller but also by interspersing current political news-reports and his personal observations on world history, in the story. Given this understanding, this politics of understatement is a let-down.

NOTES

1. Salman Rushdie, *Shame* (Bombay: Rupa, 1983).
2. Siddhartha Varadarajan, "Media and Empire; World News through the Colonial Gaze," *The Times of India*, Oct. 24, 1996.
3. Frantz Fanon, *The Wretched of the Earth* (Middlessex: Penguin, 1985), pp. 32-33.
4. Hans Kohn, *Nationalism: Its Meaning and History* (Princeton: Anvil, 1965), pp. 16-18, 46, 50-54.
5. See also Ashis Nandy, *The Illegitimacy of Nationalism: Rabindranath Tagore and the Politics of Self* (Delhi: Oxford University Press, 1994).

Enslaving Readings: Salman Rushdie's *The Satanic Verses* and Textuality[1]

JOEL KUORTTI

Rushdie, I presume, has become another kind of Livingstone which the reader sets out to find in the thicket of texts on the "Rushdie Affair,"[2] only being buried alive deeper and deeper as the texts grow in number.

Suddenly, soon after its publication in September 1988, *The Satanic Verses*[3] caused a mutual revulsion of rival groups of readers. This offensive revulsion is most often interpreted as fundamental difference between the secular West and the Muslim Orient. For example, Syed Shahabuddin, who initiated a ban on the novel in India, writes in an open letter to Rushdie in *The Times of India* in October 1988 in the following way: "Call us primitive, call us fundamentalists, call us superstitious barbarians, call us what you like, but your book only serves to define what has gone wrong with the Western civilization,"[4] and, as an afterword to an incident where a copy of the book had been burnt in Bradford, UK, Rushdie writes in *The Observer* in January 1989 that "the zealot protests serve to confirm, in the Western mind, all the worst stereotypes of the Muslim world."[5] These two incidents, the ban and the book burning,[6] or rather the way they are explicated, have been two major aspects in this discourse of mutual revulsion or offence.

The publicized texts on both the banning and the burning of *The Satanic Verses* first structured *The Satanic Verses* affair as a controversy, or a war,[7] drawing the battle line between East (most of all Islam) and West, or even further, between Believers and Atheists.[8] This divide is later emphasized by other texts drawing from various passions. In the following I discuss the affair through on the one hand some Muslim and on the other some liberal or secular points of view. There are different lines of thought in both of these main divisions,[9] but I do not attempt a classification of these here. Rather I cling onto the self-assertion of the texts of them being either-or. As the number of texts to choose from amounts to 'one thousand and one plus one' my choice remains necessarily more like arbitrary than representative. Although the coherence of these different stances is fictional, the *imperatives of argument* do seem to fall into patterns.

The discourse of mutual revulsion in general is described by Albert Hirschman to be "shaped, not so much by fundamental personality traits, but simply by the *imperatives of argument*, almost regardless of the desires, character, or convictions of the participants."[10] This means that the argumentation stems from the linguistically embedded internal logic of the arguments, rather than from the intentions of the arguers. This is one thing which is "enslaving" in the readings of *The Satanic Verses*: the imperatives of argument—mutually just as unacceptable, offensive—which dictate, or rather, predict the discussion. The application of these imperatives can be described to be unintentional (or unconscious) as for example in an immediate reaction, politically (or culturally) informed as for example in a contemplated article, or underlined (or enforced) as for example in an official decree or edict. All of these categories have been used to explain the affair. There have been some attempts to understand more fully each others's ideological contingencies but something hinders the resulting consensus.[11]

The Satanic Verses can be seen as a dislocated text. It is dislocated in its material, in its reception, and in its *generic space*.[12] Materially this suggests that the narrative refers to multiple historical and textual material and combines them in different, dislocated, new contexts. So, it is a "novel" at least in that sense, in being new. This reflects "the electric, hybridized nature of the Indian artistic tradition" sketched in *The Satanic Verses:* "The Mughals had brought artists from every part of India to work on the paintings; individual identity was submerged to create a many-headed, many-brushed Overartist who, literally, *was* Indian painting." (70; Rushdie's emphasis)

When the text opens up (into) such a hybrid tradition, it is perhaps no wonder to find even further diversity in its reception. In reception, the dislocation means that readers have found the book to be very different things, to stand for various ideological positions, and that readers insist the *others* are wrong in their perception. It is in this *insistence* that *The Satanic Verses* becomes *dis*-located, not that it would otherwise be located correctly, but having no one specific location. When it comes to its generic space, displacement is also a mode of being "new English" or "English" literature—"at a slight angle to reality," to use a phrase from *Shame* by Rushdie.[13] The immense problems of cultural translation are inherent in a varied literature like this, perhaps most of all the question of authenticity. These dislocations have given reason to several of the most severe critiques against the novel and its author: that it perverts the history, tradition, and truth, that it is directed at a Western audience in order to determinately vilify Muslims, and that its author is himself a deranged or deracinated person.[14]

Due to the controversiality, what is at stake in *The Satanic Verses* affair is also an attempt at affirmation of (communal) identity against another, dreaded community. What is meant by the terms 'Muslim' or 'fundamentalist' and 'liberal' or 'secular' turns out to be one of the key questions in the debate over *The Satanic Verses*. Each term is for the believer or promoter a positive and for the critic or opponent an ambiguous, even negative definition. A lot of the debate evolves around these themes of definition and self-definition. There is a tendency to perceive the other as enslaving, blind, one-sided, and oneself as the 'true,' right-minded, in a way which often seems naive, even callous. A strong argument against this tendency is put by Zeenat Vakil, a character in *The Satanic Verses*: "Why should there be a good, right way of being a wog? That's Hindu fundamentalism. Actually, we're all bad Indians. Some worse than others."(52)[15]

The confrontation between the Muslim and Western cultures

is by no means created by *The Satanic Verses* affair. It is a debate going back to the birth of Islam and is described lately in such broad terms as 'Orientalism' on the one hand and 'fundamentalism' on the other. The perceived threat of losing one's identity is clearly part of the arguments. The West, in this case especially Britain, is afraid of a growing Muslim community,[16] which correspondingly is afraid of losing its identity in a hostile and alien environment.[17] These fears are old, too, and they escalate in the accusations of conspiracies, which are enacted also in context of this affair: whether it is an Islamic fundamentalist plot funded by Saudis and other Gulf states,[18] or whether it is an international (Zionist) conspiracy.[19] Offence is given and taken on both sides of the invisible divide. The interpretation of the "Beyond" or "Behind," of "what is *really* the issue," is indeed a starting point for much of the writing,[20] and so Shabbir Akhtar suggests that "it is helpful to include in this list the possibility that the [Muslim] outrage is authentic. After all, it is unwise to list every possible explanation other than the true one." (55) On the other hand, considering the accusations against *The Satanic Verses* for it being blasphemous, *The New Republic* writes that "we know about the debt that democracy owes to heresy," and that "blasphemy . . . is a birthpang of democracy."[21] Only a portion of the writing tends to move on even beyond the 'beyond' of this confrontation.[22]

Presumably one of the main reasons why many people have been puzzled over the debate is the insecurity about authority: "who is repressing the authentic voice of my conviction in public." The debate undoubtedly suffers from biased publicity by Muslims and Westerners alike, though the Muslim voice is very much subdued, and even more so in the first phase of the controversy, especially in Britain, then the main stage of the affair. Manazir Ahsan and A.R. Kidwai, for example, insist that the "authentic Muslim point of view" and "genuine Muslim anger" have been "misdirected to issues of freedom of speech and censorship."[23] Aziz Al-Azmeh, too, comments on the question of authenticity, saying that "[a]t issue therefore are political questions of authority. What is at issue is who represents Muslims and who speaks in their name on a range of questions." (17) The issue of freedom of expression, which is interpreted and defined in a great variety of ways during the debate, lies on the opposite end of the line of argument. In a similar representative manner it is put forward as the genuine core of liberal and secular West's self-identity, though not without grudges from different directions.

On 14 February 1989 the matters are further confused, for then the Ayatollah Khomeini pronounces his *fatwa*, a religious sentence, in this case a death sentence.[24] This edict releases a new fervor of arguments, as it expands the issue to a wider international political arena. Khomeini's sentence is seen also as a part of Iranian internal politics,[25] in the same way as Shahabuddin's insistence on the ban in India, and the Muslim politicians's activity in Britain and Pakistan, all are accused of playing for the vote.[26] One consequence is that the Muslim argument becomes less integrated, as many "moderate" Muslims, for example the Saudis, do not validate Khomeini's edict, or are opposed to it.[27]

It turns out, too, that now it is the whole of Western civilization in danger, if one is to believe the editorials, letters, and articles in Western media from that time. The excessive unproportioned reaction for which the Muslim response had been severely criticized, gets its Western equivalent. Bhikhu Parekh writes: "It was depressing to note how the legitimate rage against the Ayatollah's murderous impertinence and outrageous Muslim support for it escalated step by even sillier step to a wholly mindless anger against all *Bradford* Muslims, then against all *British* Muslims, then against all *Muslims*, and ultimately against *Islam* itself. . . . The neutral observers were left wondering on which side of the debate lay 'fundamentalism,' 'medievalism' and 'intolerance.'"[28] Parekh's observation is sharp as he summarizes in his article how the British press treated or even "engineered" *The Satanic Verses* affair (77) following "a sad and predictable pattern." The imperatives of argument predicted the course of events to such an extent that many writers express their doubt in the sincerity of either one of the extremes. Parekh continues: "The history of the last one thousand years . . . was tragicomically re-enacted before our eyes, and its white and brown *dramatis personae* parroted well-worn lines of their banal roles in all too familiar accents." (79-80, his emphases) These roles are enacted so nearly with the certainty of a natural law, that all efforts to settle the question seem to be futile. When one is dealing with *The Satanic Verses* affair, it is difficult to dismiss the juridical concepts such as natural law. They are invoked in so much of the writing on it: there are, among other things, the bans, there is the fatwa, and there is the argument over blasphemy laws and censorship, especially in Britain. Many forensic metaphors and allegories have been used, too. Why is it so? What is in here that lends itself so easily to the forensic rhetoric? One aspect here could well be at least that to put forward a legitimate case in court would strengthen one's argument. Both parties seem to regard the foundation of one's juridical position as guaranteed by something equalling natural law. Here I can only illustrate this with a couple of considerations. One of the first striking features in the debate is the disagreement on the generic space of *The Satanic Verses*: what is this piece of writing? Is it just fiction, is it just a racist pamphlet, is it just historical distortion, or is it something else?[29]

In the West, the principle of "being able to say everything"[30] is a kind of license warranted by the writers; this is of course only a principle which is frequently violated. The Muslim arguments most often deny the validity of this principle,[31] and promote another definition: freedom of expression "through a sound chain of authority."[32] The Western principle is founded on the secular, liberal "text" of Enlightenment,[33] whereas the Muslim principle rests on the status of the Quran as infallible word of God, the ultimate text.[34] So, the question concerning the limits of literature is seen also as a test of these principles: meanwhile, *The Satanic Verses* is placed between "the end of civilization"[35] and "offend[ing] 800m Muslims."[36] I can no more than try to begin to answer that question here even if I knew that I would not succeed. In order to do so, I am contemplating the title.[37] This successive question of the title emphasizes the question about the status of a work as literature, as for example

Shahabuddin writes: "The very title of [the] book is suggestively derogatory." (48) The title of *The Satanic Verses* is indeed central to the debate in question; it already suggests the unfolding of the text.

The title of a work is, first of all, a legal "name" of it: it "names and guarantees the identity, the unity and the boundaries of the original work which it entitles"[38] and it can be used to judge various legal positions about authorship, copyright and so on.[39] The title not only marks the boundaries of a work, but it, being on the border of a work, also marks the opening which extends the work over these boundaries. Otherwise, expressions like Shahabuddin's "the very title of [the] book is suggestively derogatory" would carry no conviction. Through this opening, this law of the title as an opening, Shahabuddin links the Quran straight with *The Satanic Verses* as a derogatory comment on the Quran's status as divine revelation.

How does this come about? The satanic verses? What does the title tell us, what does it suggest? By the way of citation, the expression "satanic verses" has extended its scope of being a 'mere' name into containing a multitude of accounts. What the title of *The Satanic Verses* is citing (124) and the narrative of the novel relating (among other things) (114-25) is another, very much disputed,[40] account also called "Satanic Verses" (Hadith al-Gharaniq), which is about alleged interpolation in the Quran. Ali Mazrui writes about this and connects it, more explicitly than Shahabuddin with the Quran: "By the term 'Satanic verses' [Rushdie] refers to more than an alleged incident in the history of Islamic revelation. . . . [He] has . . . done his mischief of creating doubt about the authenticity of the Quran. . . ." [modifications added] (102) What this means, Mazrui further explains, is that as "the Quran is the ultimate constitution of its community of believers . . . Rushdie not only casts doubt on the authenticity of the source of that fundamental law. He also satirizes its rules." [ellipses added]

Now, here we are right in the middle of the problem, the imperative of argument which is invoked through the title: "satanic verses." The story about interpolation is itself interpolated within the title. And so both instances of the expression are interpreted to refer to and frame the same thing. The title is entitled to do this. It is the law of the title: to leave, to mark an opening to the story it also encloses. To quote Derrida: "The text bears its title and bears upon it. Would not its proper object, if it had one, be the effect produced by the play of the title? To show and veil in an ellipsis the powerful operation of the given title?" (212) The title is indeed powerful, the play of the title has been productive in providing imperatives of argument. The title "satanic verses" is not only entitled to secure the boundaries of the text, but it is at the same time a promise, or a threat, of the 'outside,' which lurks in and out through this opening.

Do we know what a title is? It has been a more powerful guardian of the text than the other "guardians (author, publisher, critics, academics, archivists, librarians, lawyers, and so on)" for it has further yielded its power to even more powerful guardians, "in particular the set of laws and social conventions that legitimatizes all these things."[41] The title at the same time shows and veils the law of the title. And it has done so in two simultaneous, seemingly opposite directions, calling for two sets of fundamental laws, or imperatives of argument. This can be illustrated by referring to the importance of *not* reading. It has been regarded as both a vice and a virtue having not read *The Satanic Verses*, to have defended it or protested against it without reading it. For example Shahabuddin writes: "Yes, I have not read [*The Satanic Verses*], nor do I intend to. I do not have to wade through a filthy drain to know what filth is." (47) And Akhtar confirms that "it is not a necessary condition of having knowledge of a work that one should have read it, any more than it is necessary for a judge to witness a murder in order to pass judgement." (Akhtar 40) Just as well it has been possible to defend the book without having read it, in *principle*.

Another, contrasting argument has been that others have not been able to read the work *in its full import*: as well as arguments for Islamic history, culture, and sensitivity this has meant arguments for Western liberalism, tolerance, and freedom.

To conclude, I think the main objective of my study is to

emphasize the importance of fighting enslaving readings, though that is anything but easy. Everyone of us has some contingencies or others, and that is perfectly alright. The simplistic, rigid positions one takes, however, are only pre-judged to be contradicted, and they also tend to ridicule oneself and others. I feel it is extremely difficult to predict how we might find a place for conflicting readings. To round this up, I shall quote a passage from *The Satanic Verses* where the counter- protagonists Gibreel and Saladin sing. Let us face the music: "Let's face it: it was impossible for them to have heard one another, much less conversed and also competed thus in song. Accelerating towards the planet, atmosphere roaring around them, how could they? But let's face this, too: they did." (6)

NOTES

1. This paper was originally delivered as a paper in the ESSE/2 conference in Bordeaux, 7 September 1993. Thanks to Nicholas Royle and Olli Unkuri for their critique and support while preparing the manuscript.
2. It is here necessary to acknowledge an uneasiness with the term with which this series of events has been labelled. I have chosen to talk about "*The Satanic Verses* affair" as it is rather *The Satanic Verses* than Salman Rushdie that is at issue, although the one used the most would be "the Rushdie affair."
3. Salman Rushdie, *The Satanic Verses* (London: Viking, 1988).
4. Syed Shahabuddin, "You Did This with Satanic Forethought, Mr. Rushdie," Letter, *The Times of India*, Oct. 13 (1988): sec. 2, p. 2, rep. in *The Rushdie File*, ed. Lisa Appignanesi and Sara Maitland (London: 4th Estate, 1989), p. 47.
5. Salman Rushdie, "Choice between Light and Dark," *The Observer*, Jan., 22 (1989), 11, rep. in *The Rushdie File* pp. 74-75.
6. "The burning of *The Satanic Verses* is therefore a warning signal of dangers to come" writes *The Economist*, "Burning Bestseller," Jan., 20 (1989), pp. 91-93.
7. "We are embattled in the war between the cultural imperatives of

Western liberalism, and the fundamentalist interpretations of Islam, both of which seem to claim an abstract and universal authority," Homi Bhabha, "Beyond Fundamentalism and Liberalism," *New Statesman and Society*, 2.39 (1989), p. 34.

8. Religious leaders of various religions have given their opinion: see *Sacrilege versus Civility: Muslim Perspectives on 'The Satanic Verses" Affair*, ed. M. Manazir Ahsan and A.R. Kidwai (Leicester: The Islamic Foundation, 1991), pp. 121-28.
9. Amir Taheri discusses some points of the variety within the Islamic response in "Reflections on an invalid *fatwa*," *Index on Consorship*, 19.4 (1990), pp. 14-16. See also Yasmin Alibhai, *New Statesman and Society*, Feb. 15 (1991), pp. 17-18. The division of the liberal stance runs roughly with the opinion on the extent of 'free speech' and 'censorship'; see e.g. the following: Roald Dahl, *The Times*, Feb. 28 (1989), p. 15, and "Two Cheers for Blasphemy," *New Republic*, 200.11 (1989), pp. 7-9.
10. Albert O. Hirschman, *The Rhetoric of Reaction: Perversity, Futility, Jeopardy* (London: UK and Cambridge, Mass.: Belknap Press, 1991), p. x.
11. See e.g. Bhabha, pp. 34-35.
12. To emphasize the variety of options allotted for the genre of *The Satanic Verses*, I have coined this term as a substitute for 'genre.' See also Jacques Derrida "The Law of Genre," trans. Avital Ronell, *Acts of Literature*, ed. Derek Attridge (New York and London: Routledge, 1992), pp. 223-52.
13. Rushdie, *Shame* (London: Picador, 1984), p. 29.
14. See e.g. Aziz Al-Azmeh, "The Satanic Flame," *New Statesman and Society*, 2.33 (1989), p. 17, and *The Rushdie File*, p. 4.
15. This is very close to what Gayatri Spivak called "ethical singularity," when she was addressing the question whether it is possible to escape the ethnographic enclosure, in the "Narratives and Narrated Subjects of Colonialism," Conference at the University of Turku, Finland, Dec. 5, 1992.
16. See the British Minister of State John Patten's letter "To Muslim Leaders in Britain," July 4 (1989), in *The Times*, July 5 (1989), p. 13, rep. in *Sacrilege versus Civility*, 321-25. This fear and its consequences are powerfully expressed in *The Satanic Verses*, in the episode of the encounter between Saladin and the immigration officers, see pp. 139-42 and 157-69.

17. See Shabbir Akhtar, *Be Careful with Muhammad: The Salman Rushdie Affair* (London: Bellew, 1989), p. 7. There is also an episode in *The Satanic Verses* where these fears are expressed through another character, Hind, see pp. 245-51.
18. See e.g. Malise Ruthven, "Islam and the Book," *The Times Literary Supplement*, 4469 (1988), p. 1312, or Aziz Al-Azmeh, p. 73.
19. See translations of broadcasts by Tehran home service, President Khamene'i, and Ayatollah Khomeini in *BBC Summary of World Broadcasts*, Feb. 17, 20 and 24 (1989), rep. in *The Rushdie File*, pp. 85-87, 89, 90.
20. See e.g. the review of *The Satanic Verses* in *Kayhan Farangi*, "Rushdie Has Fallen into Total Moral Degradation," Dec. 1988, translated in *The Independent*, Feb. 21 (1989), p. 12, rep. in *The Rushdie File*, p. 24.
21. "Two Cheers for Blasphemy," p. 7.
22. See Bhabha, p. 35.
23. Muhammad Manazir Ạhsan and A.R. Kidwai, "Muslim Perspective," *Sacrilege versus Civility*, p. 25. Akhtar criticizes harshly the choice of interviewees on the affair, see Akhtar, pp. 41-51. Only after some time, he writes, "[o]ne began to hear authentic Muslim voices on the radio and see Muslim faces on the television with some regularity. The so-called moderate Muslims and others whose orthodoxy was suspect were being gradually phased out," p. 51.
24. Ayatollah Ruhollah Khomeini, Radio Tehran, 14 Feb. 1989, in *Kayhan Havai*, 22 Feb. 1989, in *The Rushdie File*, p. 84: "the author of the book *The Satanic Verses*, which has been compiled, printed, and published in opposition to Islam, the Prophet and the Koran, as well as those publishers who were aware of its contents, have been sentenced to death." The complex juridical and theological considerations of the position of Khomeini's *fatwa* in Islamic jurisprudence are not dealt with in here.
25. See Amir Taheri, "Khomeini's Scapegoat," *The Times*, Feb. 15 (1989), p. 14, rep. in *The Rushdie File*, pp. 94-95.
26. See Al-Azmeh, p. 17, and GPD, "Blackmail Works" in *Economical and Political Weekly*, 23:43, Oct. 22 (1988), p. 2199, rep. in *The Rushdie File*, pp. 51-52. Also Akhtar admits that it "is not to deny that many Muslims have, as in Pakistan, exploited the Rushdie furore purely for their own personal political ends," p. 54.

27. E.g. Zaki Badawi, chairman of the Imams and Mosques Council, and of the Islamic Law Council, writes "with all the authority under my command that anyone who seeks or incites anyone to kill Rushdie is committing a crime against God and the Islamic *shari'a*." "Spurn the Book, Spare the Man: Interview with Paul Martin," *The Guardian*, Feb. 27 (1989), p. 39.
28. Bhikhu Parekh, "The Rushdie Affair and the British Press," *Salman Rushdie Controversy in Interreligious Perspective*, ed. Dan Cohn-Sherbok (Lewiston: Edwin Mellen, 1990), p. 79.
29. In terms of Jacques Derrida's essay "Before the Law," one could ask about *The Satanic Verses*, are we dealing with a literary text? In other words: "Who decides, who judges, and according to what criteria, that this relation [this account] belongs [or does not belong] to literature?" ("Before the Law," trans. Avital Ronell, in *Acts of Literature*, p. 187, modifications added). The choice of judges and criteria is decisive. And as there is no consensus on these questions, it is anything but clear what is being referred to when the word 'literature' is mentioned in this debate. The conflict between the communities of subjects participating in the affair seems to be based on them *not* being "in the same culture" and *not* subscribing, in the context of *The Satanic Verses*, "to the same system of conventions" concerning a literary text, p. 184.
30. See "This Strange Institution Called Literature: Interview with Jacques Derrida," *Acts of Literature*, pp. 40-41.
31. So e.g. Akhtar writes: "In the United Kingdom we have laws restricting by common consent many excesses in the freedom of expression . . . the question here is about the *limits* of this outrage. According to English law, what is not prohibited is permitted; but many things are explicitly prohibited. . . . There are disputes, sometimes intractable, about the precise definition of the offences [sic] involved, but the underlying principles are universally accepted," pp. 55-56.
32. Ahsan and Kidwai, p. 27.
33. "Two Cheers for Blasphemy," p. 8.
34. Ali A. Mazrui, "*The Satanic Verses* or a Satanic Novel? Moral Dilemmas of the Rushdie Affair," *Alternatives* 25 (1990), pp. 100-3.
35. Amos Oz, in "Words for Salman Rushdie," *The New York Times Book Review,* Mar. 12 (1989), pp. 1 & 28-29.
36. Ahsan and Kidwai, p. 52.

37. Cf. Derrida's fourth axiom in "Before the Law": "We think we know what a title is, notably the title of a work," p. 188.
38. Derrida, "Before the Law," p. 188.
39. That this has not always been so, is another question which I will not go into here.
40. See Ahsan, "The 'Satanic' Verses and the Orientalists," *Sacrilege verses Civility*, pp. 131-41.
41. "Before the Law," p. 214.

Intercultural Identification and Salman Rushdie's *The Satanic Verses*

JOEL KUORTTI

Martin Luther King's catch-phrase, "I have a dream," speaks not only about idealism but also about commitment, I, too, have a dream, that in the future our work will make the dream come true. Dreams, how are they relevant to *The Satanic Verses* and the debate over it? In their multiple forms, dreams can be seen as forming a structure for the novel and the debate: there are ideals and goals, fantasies and desires, illusions and aspirations. These dreams can be nightmares, too, as in the passage where Saladin Chamcha, one of the novel's double protagonists, has a nightmare in which he feels sorry for the people of colour: "Every morning you have to look at yourself in the mirror and see, staring back, the darkness, the stain, the proof that you're the lowest of the low."[1] Waking up, Chamcha realizes that he himself is seen with such a stain, too: "Dreams put things in their own way; but Chamcha . . . was bitterly aware that the nightmare had not been so far from the truth; the spirit, at least, was right." (256)

The position in which Rushdie writes is not without similar complications. Multiple allegiances are expected, if not professed, as well as multiple sources. It is therefore not surprising that his work should be regarded differently by different critics. So, for example, Edward Said writes: "Before *The Satanic Verses* appeared in 1988, Rushdie was already a problematic figure for the English, thanks to his essays and earlier novels; to many Indians and Pakistanis in England and the subcontinent, however, he was not only a celebrated author they were proud of but also a champion of immigrants' rights and a severe critic of nostalgic imperialism."[2] That this is so does not mean that he was unproblematic for Indians and Pakistanis as well, but as Said, too, notes, "After the *fatwa* his status changed drastically, and he become anathema to his former admirers." (373) It is not only the work, *The Satanic Verses*, however, which has caused the continuing dilemma. Homi Bhabha raises the important question concerning "the unreadness of the book," important from the beginning of the debate, and that question is: "Where is the book being authored from?"[3] Bhabha distinguishes here three sites of authoring: the racial situation, the Iranian situation, and the literati. The first two most often take up the disguise of Muslim position and the last the Western mask.

What has to be kept constantly in mind when looking at such complex issues as the question above is, that there is no one position in the affair which can be located as the "Western" or the "Muslim" position. There is a multitude of these positions with agreements on some points and disagreement on others.[4] My aim is specifically at an evaluation of some of these positions, how they are structured and how they argue for their claims on what I call the three levels of dreams.

The first level of dream is that of revelation, which is the point of departure also for the novel, both in its title and its theme. On this level we encounter one of the most difficult questions put forward in the whole debate: what does the book say about the revelation and more specifically about the Quran?

The historical-critical method, which has been applied to the Bible studies for about a century, has not been used in the Quran studies, there is for example no critical edition of the Quran. So the interpretative models available and applied in *The Satanic Verses* affair within these religious and cultural traditions are significantly different. What does this imply?

Every second chapter of *The Satanic Verses* is a revelation in the form of a dream of Gibreel Farishta, the other one of the double protagonists. The miracle of revelation, its possibility, nature, and meaning, all this is studied in the context of a modern society, modern interpretations, modern attitudes, and so on. The possibility of revelation is not directly rejected. What follows is maybe the most effective aspect of this: the problematization of the reconciliation of the contemporary experience of revelation with the surrounding world. Gibreel fears sleep, because he does not know how to interpret his experience; it is not just the psychic disorder the doctors diagnose as paranoid schizophrenia. (429) But as such a method in general is not applicable in Islamic ideology to the Quran as the ultimate text and to the Prophet as the ideal person, the episodes are interpreted in a different way than in the Western readings.

This leads onto the second level of dreams, the level of cultural contact, where the allegiances are again tested. The double protagonists Saladin Chamcha and Gibreel Farishta act out several polarities, but the themes of good and evil, true and false, continuous and discontinuous, are treated in a way which does not allow any easy preferences for ethical judgements. Especially continuity and discontinuity of identities in a migrant situation are central themes of the novel, emphasized in cultural contact.

The character of Saladin portrays one of the migrant positions, that of a conformist. His dream city is "ellowen deeowen," London (37), which turns into a nightmare, into something which "hadn't been Chamcha's way; not his, nor that of the England he had idolized and come to conquer." (270) Not without persistence and success in becoming Anglicized, Chamcha is nevertheless betrayed by his dream city.

> Had he not pursued his own idea of *the good*, sought to become that which he most admired, dedicated himself with a will bordering and obsession to the conquest of Englishness? (256)

There is also no simple turning back and Chamcha, being as perplexed with his disillusionment as Gibreel is with his dreams, accepts the hybridity of his identity. (288-89) In his consideration of the concept of the hybrid identity, Ziauddin Sardar explains Rushdie's positions as "a residue of the Orientalist tradition," in which the "brown sahib has an acute inferiority complex about his original identity."[5] Sardar writes in the vein of what Akbar Ahmed defines as radical Islam[6] and he is opposed to the idea of hybridity, promoting authenticity instead.

There is, though, a strong critical argument against simplicist appraisals of the West in *The Satanic Verses*. This is manifest in the anti-Thatcher figure of Maggie which is burnt, (293) in the descriptions of brutality by the immigration officers, (157-71) and by the police. (449-51) They are not only disillusioned comments on society, but provide the third platform of authoring the novel: the racial situation in the Western civilization. In his wife Pamela's dream, Chamcha prophetizes an end to this civilization:

> "Things are ending," he told her. "This civilization; things are closing in on it. It has been quite a culture, brilliant and foul, cannibal and Christian, the glory of the world. We should celebrate it while we can; until night falls." (184)

This dream is at the same time both ironic and perceptive, bearing in mind the double-bind of cultural contact.

With its perceived closeness to the Islamic tradition and the Quran, *The Satanic Verses* has posed serious interpretative problems to Muslims as well as to other readers. In this the most painful aspect for all is perhaps the fight over identities. What is an identity in the global, multinational, multi-ethic, multi-faith world? On a market of exchange where the rates have not been fixed? When the definitions of self clash, there are inevitably conflicts. Akbar Ahmed, as a Muslim anthropologist living in the West commenting on the lack of hope of dialogue, says: "In this atmosphere, even to hint at dispassionate analysis of the situation was to risk being labelled disloyal to the cause, a traitor to the community." (171) Ahmed's book, *Postmodernism and Islam*, is a very critical undertaking, too, studying the varying Muslim positions, as well as taking a similar approach to Western ones, and he sees that the problem of identity is not only with the individual, but it is also a communal matter.

As a communal matter, Rushdie's book has been described

as blasphemous in both negative and positive terms. David Lawton gives a short definition of blasphemy in his book by the same name: "Blasphemy is an exchange—a conversation gone wrong."[7] In *The Satanic Verses* affair, the conversation has gone wrong very deeply, reinforcing the intercultural conflicts, marking the ruptures of communities. Lawton also links the problematics of blasphemy with the question of identity: "It is plausible, I think, *The Satanic Verses* function as blasphemy in the Freudian mode, blasphemy as the ostensible structure of the narrative answering to blasphemy as writer's own coding of identity." (179) Thus blasphemy is a positive term for negative identification with the orthodoxy. For blasphemy, Lawton continues, "is an orthodoxy's way of demonising difference in order to perpetrate violence against it . . . assuring orthodoxy of its own identity." (202) And so Nasim Ansari, for example, writes that "Rushdie's fiction raises interesting issues of belief and skepticism that are provocative but not really blashphemous, unless one starts from the premise that the very shadow of a doubt on holiness is blasphemous."[8]

There are, in fact, descriptions which allow Rushdie's prose critical value with regard to the blasphemy charges. The editorial "Two Cheers for Blasphemy" claims that "blasphemy is nothing to be ashamed about. It is a birthpang of democracy."[9] The kind of examples from Sardar to "Two Cheers for Blasphemy" tend to employ the most used device in cultural exchange, stereotypical characterization and it would be of great importance to study in detail these images produced in the debate, and to learn from that, because otherwise we easily remain on the level of stereotypes.

So we are on the third level of dreams, the level of fictionality. The "fundamentalist and intolerant Islam" is a fiction, just as well as the "secular, nihilistic West" is a fiction. When "everyone, black brown white, had started thinking of the dream-figure as *real*," (288) of paramount importance is the dismantling of these fictions and replacing them with another, the dream of a sincere dialogue. Here I would like to spend some time to look at the term 'fundamentalism.' How do you react to fundamentalism, especially Islamic fundamentalism, recurrently discussed in the media? Do you regard it, as did NATO's former secretary-general Willy Claes, as a primer risk?[10]

It is quite clear that very few would designate themselves as fundamentalists, while subscribing to the tenets proclaimed or observed in the various movements or groups named as 'fundamentalist.'[11] Thus, even though Nazih Ayubi maintains that the term has been "superimposed on to the Muslim world," he admits that going back to the sources "is a tendency to which fundamentalists of all religions incline, except that in its Islamic variety it also seems to adhere strongly to a holistic, comprehensive notion of Islam, better expressed by the term *integrisme*."[12] The terminological debate is not unimportant, for it displays the power-relations, the power of description, which underline the issue. It is a question of whose images we live by.

The perceived threat of losing one's identity is clearly part of the arguments in *The Satanic Verses* Affair. The fears are old, too, going back to the birth of Islam, and they escalate in the accusations of conspiracies which are enacted also in the context of this affair: whether it is an Islamic fundamentalist plot funded by Saudis and other Gulf states,[13] or whether it is an international (Zionist) conspiracy.[14] Offecne is given and taken on both sides of the invisible divide.

Connecting the term *integrisme* with Christianity,[15] Seyyed Hossein Nasr explains that it is a more apt term "because it refers to the views of those traditional Catholics who wish to integrate all of life into their religion and, conversely, their religion into all aspects of life."[16] Now, to talk about this ideal of synthesis is not altogether extraordinary even for the non-Muslim West, as Islamic fundamentalism has been seen in the Western media foremost as a *political* force (with Iran's Islamic revolution as the supreme example, or more recently the Afghan Taleban), aimed at reforming all of life. As such, it certainly addresses far more varied spheres than mere theological issues; it aims at reestablishing history and the present. In his study of the multiple forms of Islamic reality, *Recognizing Islam*, Michael Gilsenan expresses this delicately: "one of the most important elements in what is often called Islamic fundamentalism is precisely this struggle over the definition of what is the tradition. This means not only a religious interpretation but a whole form of life."[17]

If we read the texts from the beginning of *The Satanic Verses* affair, we can see how the issue of Islamic fundamentalism was brought about. In one of the very first reviews, the review by Madhu Jain in *India Today*, *The Satanic Verses* is referred to as "an uncompromising, unequivocal attack on religious fanaticism and fundamentalism, which in this book is largely Islamic. It makes V.S. Naipaul's *Among the Believers* [1981][18] seem like an OK certificate for Islamic fundamentalism."[19] This comparison is quite indicative of the sentiments towards many postcolonial writers. There are, at the same time, feeling of pride and contempt, appreciation and suspicion. Any criticism of the cultures of origin can easily be seen as patronizing, as espousing Western attitudes. This applies also to the criticism of Islam, and Rushdie, answering in Jain's interview to the question whether he feared "a backlash from the mullahs," says: "Even *Shame* was attacked by fundamentalist Muslims. I cannot censor. I write whatever there is to write."[20]

The undefined usage of the word 'fundamentalism' has accorded it such a widespread validity that it is quite impossible to discern what it means in any single context. When, after *The Satanic Verses* is banned in India (October 5, 1988), Rushdie sends an open letter to Prime Minister Rajiv Gandhi, he calls those Indian MPs who attacked his novel "extremists, even fundamentalists" and claims that "it's the fundamentalists who now control the political agenda in India."[21] Shahabuddin, whom Rushdie foremost criticizes, replies in his turn: "Call us primitive, call us fundamentalists, call us superstitious barbarians, call us what you like, but your book only serves to define what has gone wrong with the Western civilization."[22] It is explicitly a reaction to what Rushdie had written, and clearly Shahabuddin and the others who worked for the ban "did not like what they had read of the book."[23]

In understanding the issue of Islamic fundamentalism in *The*

Satanic Verses affair, it is also important to notice that there have been arguments saying that "this struggle over the definition of what is the tradition," perceived as fundamentalism, has been a reaction against modernism as something foreign, imported, and colonial; Shahabuddin, for example, refers to *The Satanic Verses* as "social turmoil of foreign origin." (45) And not only that, Gilsenan attributes the growth of Islamic fundamentalism to "a global expansion in the role and contradictions of the petit bourgeoisie." (263) So, the issue cannot be seen purely as a (post) colonial question, but also as a class matter, for the ideology of modernism, as Gilsenan points out, "can be stigmatized by workers and petit bourgeoisie alike as part of a mere class manipulation by the culturally privileged." (263) What we have here is, then, a complex set of suppositions converging in the term 'fundamentalism': the etymological history, the political superimposition, and the ideological accommodation.

One form of the ideological accommodation of the term 'fundamentalism' in *The Satanic Verses* affair can be found in Shabbir Akhtar's "Whose Light, Whose Darkness?" The article argues strongly, although not very clearly or sytematically, "for fundamentalist options in religion."[24] Akhtar's is a scathing criticism of the Western interpretations of the 'Rushdie affair,' and he asks if it is not so that "each and every Western writer, including so-called Islamic writers patronized by the establishment" have precisely reduced "the Rushdie affair . . . to a simple neo-Victorian opposition between our light and their darkness." (21)[25] Against this, he offers another antagonism, that of the superiority of Islam over Christianity (or the Western mind):

> The continual blasphemies against the Christian faith have totally undermined it. Any faith which compromises its internal temper of militant wrath is destined for the dustbin of history. . . . In this matter, the Koran is to have the last word: God does not guide a people who sell his signs for a paltry price. . . . The Rushdie affair is, in the last analysis, certainly about fanaticism on behalf of God. (21)

Whereas Akhtar tries to justify the fundamentalist stance, Tariq Modood asserts, in direct reference to Akhtar's statements, "that Muslim anger does not owe anything to (what I call) fundamentalism." He classifies three tendencies among the British Muslims (of South Asian origin): "Deobandi apolitical conservative revivalists, Barelvi devotionalists with a pro-British Raj history, and a small network of Saudi-backed middle class fundamentalists."[26] He sees the alleged fundamentalism of Muslims as a racist stereotype. (155) Also, attributing the Muslim outrage to fundamentalists and the mullahs is, in his opinion, racism because "[v]irtually every practising Muslim was offended by passages from the book." (154) Modood argues that the inability of the Anglicized middle/intellectual class of the Asian intelligentsia to disconnect themselves from the popular Western stereotypes and to "understand and/or feel responsible for its own ethnic working-class is . . . the single most worrying trend in the Muslim and other Asian communities." (155)

Although the word 'fundamentalism' is invoked in *The Satanic Verses* affair, it remains a problematic term. Fazlur Rahman distinguishes four groups of Muslims: "the secularist, the modernist, the traditionalist, and the neo-fundamentalist."[27] Of these, traditionalists are closest to the kind of 'conservatives' who in a Christian context could be called 'fundamentalists.' The neo-fundamentalists, then, are perhaps closest to what is usually understood with the general term 'fundamentalist.' In Ayubi's words, they "are often splinter groups from the larger fundamentalist gatherings, and are usually more radical or militant in orientation. They tend on the whole to be more eclectic in their selection and in their reading of the authoriative sources, and they are generally more inclined towards *immediate* action of one sort or another." (68, Ayubi's emphasis) This observation, apart from the fact that it is precisely *militancy* which characterizes Western media coverage of fundamentalism, makes a very intriguing partial definition of 'Islamic fundamentalism,' pointing out its selectivity in choosing the texts it uses as a basis for its beliefs. In this, as Richard Antoun describes it, fundamentalism "represents a sharp break with established religious tradition at the same time that it calls for a return to the past."[28] Rushdie, too, notes of the fundamentalists that "[t]heir extremism is actually something new."[29]

In a peculiar way, Islamic fundamentalism becomes a proponent of postmodernism, carving out for itself what Homi Bhabha, in another context, calls an "in-between" space "for elaborating strategies of selfhood—singular or communal—that initiate new signs of identity, and innovative sites of collaboration, and contestation, in the act of defining the idea of society itself."[30] True enough, Rahman describes this "modern, richer version of fundamentalism" as "postmodernist and [it] has been influenced by modernism," (32) and Ahmed also argues that "ethno-religious revivalism is both cause and effect of postmodernism." (13) There is both a contestation *of* modernism and a relation *with* (post) modernism in Islamic fundamentalism. While Youssef Choueiri maintains that for fundamentalism to lay stress on "a creative interpretation of its revealed text . . . is thoroughly uncritical, apologetic, and didactic,"[31] the relation remains, whatever the approach is, and this relation is a striking one.

Fictionality has not only to do with the stereotypes. There is no unanimity with regard to *The Satanic Verses* on this point either. Is it fictional, does it have a "critical function," is it malicious? Jacques Derrida discusses this point of *The Satanic Verses* affair in the following way:

> What we call literature (not belles-letters or poetry) implies that license is given to the writer to say everything he wants to or everything he can, while remaining shielded, safe from all censorship, be it religious or political. . . . The freedom to say everything is a very powerful political weapon, but which might immediately let itself be neutralized as a fiction.[32]

Derrida criticizes the ambiguity of this critical function of literature in the West considering especially the institution of censorship. For an intercultural issue, these questions are even more acute. Rather than reading the text as mere fiction, we shall have to take into account what Bhabha defined in the words by Lawton:

> The key importance of the Rushdie affair for professional students like myself is that it demonstrates, once and for all, the inadequacy of the model of reading we have maintained for too long: the individual reader, the supposedly 'private' reader, reading the individual text. A study of blasphemy is therefore relevant to finding a better model, one that engages with communities, something rival collectivities, and diverse cultural and cross-cultural positioning. (7)

To conclude, *The Satanic Verses* affair can help us to reveal the agency through which we shape our identities, the dreams we live by. Maybe, within the intercultural exchange, we can find more appropriate ways to do this. "The night guards often doze off. . . . That's how we manage to get to talk." (167)

NOTES

1. Salman Rushdie, *The Satanic Verses* (London: Viking, 1988), p. 255.
2. Edward W. Said, *Culture and Imperialism* (London: Chatto and Windus, 1993), p. 373.
3. Homi Bhabha, "Postcolonial Authority and Postmodern Guilt," in *Cultural Studies*, ed. Lawrence Grossberg, Cary Nelson, and Paula Treichler (New York and London: Routledge, 1992), pp. 66-67.
4. See John L. Esposito, *The Islamic Threat: Myth or Reality?* (New York and Oxford: Oxford University Press, 1992), p. 192, and James Piscatori, "The Rushdie Affair and the Politics of Ambiguity," *International Affairs*, 66: 4 (1990), pp. 779-80.
5. Ziauddin Sardar, "The Rushdie Malaise: A Critique of Some Writing on the Rushdie Affair," *Muslim World Book Review*, 10:3 (1990), pp. 3-17. Repr. in *Sacrilege Versus Civility: Muslim Per-*

spectives on The Satanic Verses Affair, pp. 279 and 281.

6. Akbar S. Ahmed, *Postmodernism and Islam: Predicament and Promise* (London and New York: Routledge, 1992), pp. 159-63.
7. David Lawton, *Blasphemy* (Hemel Hempstead: Harvester Wheatsheaf, 1993), p. 5.
8. Nasim Ansari, "Blasphemy and Religious Criticism," *Economic and Political Weekly*, 27:27, 4 July 1992, p. 1383.
9. Salman Rushdie, "Two Cheers for Blasphemy," Editorial, *New Republic*, 200: 11, 13 Mar. 1989, p. 7.
10. Willy Claes, "Transatlantic Rift Haunts Nato," Interview with Andrew Marshall, *The Independent*, 8 Feb. 1995, p. 12.
11. R. Hrair Dekmeijan claims, however, the following: "Proponents and sympathizers [of the heightening of Islamic consciousness] frequently use the following expression: *baath al-Islami* (Islamic renaissance), *sahwah al-Islamiyyah* (Islamic awakening), *usuliyyah al-Islamiyyah* (Islamic fundamentalism). The most appropriate form is *al-usuliyyah al-Islamiyyah*, since it connotes a search for the fundamental of the faith, the foundations of the Islamic polity (*ummah*), and the bases of legislative authority (*al-shariyyah al-hukm*)," *Islam in Revolution* (Syracuse, New York: Syracuse University Press, 1985), p. 4.
12. Nazih N. Ayubi, *Political Islam: Religion and Politics in the Arab World* (London: Routledge, 1991), p. 68.
13. See for example Malise Ruthven, Salman Rushdie, "Islam and the Book," *The Times Literary Supplement*, 4469, 25 Nov. (1988), p. 1312, or Aziz Al-Azmeh, "The Satanic Flame," *New Statesman and Society*, 2:33, 20 Jan. 1989, p. 7.
14. See speeches by Majlis speaker Hashemi Rafsanjani, "Iran Majlis Speaker Says Publication of *The Satanic Verses* Was 'Worse than Officially Declared War,'" Speech, 15 Feb. 1989; Khamene'i Ali, "Iranian President's Sermon at Friday Prayers Attacks British Policy on *The Satanic Verses* Issue," Sermon, 17 Feb. 1989; broadcast by Tehran home service, translated subsequently in *BBC Summary of Word Broadcasts*, 17, 20 and 24 Feb. 1989, repr. in *The Rushdie File*, ed. Lisa Appignanesi and Sara Maitland (London: 4th Estate, 1989), pp. 84-86, 87-88 and 89-91.
15. 'Fundamentalism' is, after all, originally a Christian term. *Oxford English Dictionary* gives the following definition: "A religious movement, which orig. became active among various Protestant

bodies in the United States after the war 1914-1918, based on strict adherence to certain tenets (e.g. the literal inerrancy of Scripture) held to be fundamental to the Christian faith." The opposites given for this are 'liberalism' and 'modernism.' Holders of these tenets, writes Mitford M. Mathews, "began in 1921 to call themselves fundamentalists." [*A Dictionary of Americanisms* (Chicago University Press, 1951).] There is in *The Satanic Verses* also a Christian fundamentalist character, Eugene Dumsday, a creationist scientist, see *The Satanic Verses*, pp. 75-77 and 79. The word 'fundamentalism' has, however, achieved popularity and is "used to cover any manifestation of religious enthusiasm or any political intervention which has religious associations." With regard to Islam, this is true to the extent that it can now be found in almost every book and article on Islam.

16. Seyyed Hossein Nasr, *Traditional Islam in the Modern World* (1987; London and New York: Kegan Paul International, 1990), p. 304.
17. Michael Gilsenan, *Recognizing Islam: Religion and Society in the Modern Middle East* (1982; London and New York: I.B. Tauris, 1990), p. 15.
18. On Naipaul's alleged Orientalism, see Edward W. Said, *Covering Islam: How the Media and the Experts Determine How We See the Rest of the World* (London: Chatto and Windus, 1993), pp. 6-7, published before Naipaul's book *Among the Believers*. For a criticism of this allegation, see Bernard Lewis, *Islam and the West* (New York and Oxford: Oxford University Press, 1993), p. 100. The Bangladeshi writer Taslima Nasreen is another public figure who has recently engaged with this problematic. When she was receiving the Swedish PEN Award in Stockholm in August 1994, she said: "I continue to fight fundamentalism, which is spreading darkness in the world," The Finnish Broadcasting Company, TV 1, 8.30 p.m. News, 18 Aug. 1994.
19. Madhu Jain, "An Irreverent Journey: *The Satanic Verses*," *India Today*, 13:17, 15 Sep. 1988, p. 98.
20. Salman Rushdie, "My Theme is Fanaticism: Interview with Madhu Jain," *India Today*, 13:17, 15 Sep. 1998, p. 99. This is not to say that the term 'fundamentalism' only now appears in Rushdie's writing, see "In God We Trust,'" (1985) and "Mullah's Tale: *Among the Believers* by V.S. Naipaul." *The Guardian*, 1 Oct.

1981, p. 8, repr. in *Imaginary Homelands: Essays and Criticism 1981-1991* (London: Granta Books, 1991), pp. 373-75.

21. Salman Rushdie, "An Open Letter to PM Rajiv Gandhi," repr. as "Personal View," in *The Sunday Times*, 16 Oct. 1988, Sec. G, p. 4.
22. Syed Shahabuddin, "You Did This with Satanic Forethought, Mr. Rushdie," *The Times of India*, 13 Oct. 1998, Sec. 2, p. 2, repr. in *Impact International*, 18:21, 11 Nov. 1998, pp. 17-18.
23. Daniel Pipes, *The Rushdie Affair: The Ayatollah, the Novelist and the West* (New York: Birch Lane Press, 1990), p. 72.
24. Shabbir Akhtar, "Whose Light, Whose Darkness?" *The Guardian*, 27 Feb. 1989, p. 21.
25. The last part of this quotation in Akhtar's quote from W.L. Webb, "The Imam and the Scribe," p. 21. Akhtar's ellipsis.
26. See Tariq Modood, "British Asian Muslims and the Rushdie Affair," *Political Quarterly*, 61:2 (April/June 1990), p. 143, n2. See Malise Ruthven, *A Satanic Affair: Salman Rushdie and the Rage of Islam* (London: Chatto and Windus, 1990), pp. 54-80; for criticism of Ruthven, see Ahmed 129 and 183.28.
27. Fazlur Rahman, "Roots of Islamic Neo-Fundamentalism," in *Change and the Muslim World*, p. 32.
28. Richard T. Antoun, *Muslim Preacher in the Modern World: A Jordanian Case Study in Comparative Perspective* (Princeton, NJ: Princeton University Press, 1989), p. 237.
29. Salman Rushdie, "Fiction's Embattled Infidel: Interview with Gerald Marzorati," *The New York Times Magazine*, 29 Jan. 1989, p. 48.
30. Homi Bhabha, "Introduction: Locations of Culture," in *The Location of Culture* (London: Routledge, 1994), pp. 1-2. Cf. Timothy Brennan, *Salman Rushdie and the Third World* (Houndmills and London: Macmillan Press, 1989), p. x.
31. Youssef M. Choueiri, *Islamic Fundamentalism: Themes in Right-Wing Ideology and Politics Series* (London: Pinter Publisher, 1990), p. 11.
32. Jacques Derrida, *Acts of Literature*, ed. Derek Attridge (New York and London: Routledge, 1992), pp. 37-38.

A Tragic Lament beyond Postmodernist Parody: Multicultural Art's Protest against Bigoted Fundamentalism in Salman Rushdie's *The Moor's Last Sigh*

DAVID MYERS

Chaque jour vers l'Enfer nous descendons d'un pas
Baudelaire

The great problem with *The Moor's Last Sigh* is that Salman Rushdie would have liked to write a tragedy about the fall of civilization and the failure of multicultural tolerance, but because he knows that we live in an era of antiheroic farce, he could not create tragedy but only a parody of tragedy. The references to the great tragedies of both East and West are more than plentiful; they culminate in the quotations, one after the other, from the *Ramayana* and from the *Odyssey*. Both quotations narrate the hero's righteous slaying of the enemy and both quotations are filled with self-righteousness and the certainty that the human hero is the agent of God. But today, in the last decade of the twentieth century, Salman Rushdie is convinced that we live not in the tragic and mythical eras of Sita and Helen of Troy, but rather in the grubby age of commerce, mafia gang-wars and trivialising pop culture. Instead of Sita and Helen, Rushdie gives us the pageant beauty queen Nadia Wadia. As he himself says:

> And though men fought over Nadia Wadia, she was neither Helen nor Sita. Just a pretty girl in a hot spot, is all. Tragedy was not in our natures. A tragedy was taking place all

> right, a national tragedy on a grand scale, but those of us who played our parts were—let me put it bluntly—clowns. Clowns! Burlesque buffoons, drafted into history's theatre on account of the lack of greater men. Once, indeed, there were giants on our stage; but at the fag-end of an age, Madam History must make do with what she can get, Jawaharlal, in these latter days, was just the name of a stuffed dog.[1]

For Rushdie it is tragic that the multiculturalism that was once to be found in Goa and Bombay has been destroyed by a rebirth of sectarian, pseudo-religious fundamentalism. Instead of focusing on Islamic fundamentalists, however, Rushdie evokes the thuggish Ram-fundamentalists of pseudo-Hindu gangster Mainduck Fielding. When Bombay finally explodes in an Armageddon of bombs, it is partly the megalomaniacal greed of Mainduck and his arch-rival, the Moor's father-Abraham that is to blame, but equally it is the way in which the masses can be indoctrinated with a propaganda of hatred that leads inevitably to barbaric violence.

The fall of Bombay is the destruction of home, the beginning of uprootedness and the entering into hell which Rushdie equates with the loss of family roots. He locates his hell, with an emphasis on allusion to Dante, in the village of the damned, Benengeli in Portugal. At the dead centre of hell is the vulgar parvenu palace of the mediocre artist as vengeful fraud (think of the film *Amadeus* as the revenge of the mediocre artist on the genius Mozart) Vasco Miranda. The palace is the opposite of the Elefanta-palace of Aurora and of her art as masterpiece which once towered over Bombay. In this remote Portuguese village are the "human automats" the parasites, the international tourists with vacant eyes who live only to shop till they drop for international brand names; they are the living dead. In his tower of sterile pretentiousness, Vasco Miranda devotes his bloated last days to hatred and murderous revenge.

It is hardly surprising that this latest work by Salman Rushdie is marked by his painful years of solitary confinement and hiding, inflicted on him by Islamic fundamentalists since the publication of *The Satanic Verses.* I can think of no other literary work in which the grim absurdity of racial and religious hatred is illustrated not just by telling stories showing the evil of sectarian bigotry but by inventing leading characters who are never quite sure whether they are Portuguese-Catholic, Indian-Jewish, English neo-colonialist, Hindu-nationalist, Moorish, or just mixed-up freakish.

It is also hardly surprising that the satiric elan and powerful creativity which inspired his early work such as *Midnight's Children* has yielded now in *The Moor's Last Sigh* to pessimistic discourses on the failure of tolerance and of a humanist sense of mission and meaning. In the end there seems to remain only the tortured protest of the artistic work, be it an autobiography, a series of paintings, or the architecture of El-Alhambra as a pathetic reminder of the civilization that could have been if it were not for the restless human lust for power.

This is a novel which is dominated by the metaphor of the palimpsest. The characters search for the true painting which is inspired by love but it lies hidden beneath coats of varnish and a false painting inspired by megalomania and revenge. The reader searches among the strange characters for the hidden, murderous truths that lurk beneath their hypocritical, public protestations of honesty. The scholar searches for a hidden and ultimate pattern as he sifts through this work's multiracial kaleidoscope of myths, allusions, scraps of contemporary popular culture thrown in and mixed with classical images from both East and West of battles between the demigods and the historical ebb and flow of religions and cultures.

The novel's final sequence in Benengeli has become allegory. There is no road to the next village of Erasmo where philosophers debate Pascal and Erasmus. (386) The antiheroic Moor has made his final pilgrimage in his mission to find his mother's stolen paintings and to redeem himself in her memory, but he has found not redemption and heaven, but a hell produced by hatred, revenge, mediocrity, vulgarity and uprootedness. The Moor has found a cheap parody of "home" called Mooristan. The aesthetic and moral ugliness of Mooristan is allegorically contrasted with a final vision of the glory of the Alhambra, built in an age of heroism.

The Moor is the antiheroic reincarnation of his ancestor Sultan Boabdil who once at the Alhambra, five hundred years ago, failed to defend his culture and his final remaining seat of glory. Sultan Boabdil's failure becomes, through reenactment of the archetype, the failure of the Moor. The loss of courage and the loss of certainty about ethical and cultural values that must be defended to the death against the barbarians within and without are evoked by Salman Rushdie with the classical quotation: "Well may you weep like a woman . . . for what you could not defend like a man." (432) The Moor has failed to defend the artistic genius and the family reputation of his painter-mother Aurora from the jealous slander of his father Abraham, from the hysterical conspiracy of his evil mistress Uma, and from the murderous intrigues of Hindu gangboss Mainduck. He has also failed to defend the innocent Aoi Ue from murder by the heroin-addict Vasco. In her final painting before her death, Aurora Zogoiby portrays her treacherous son the Moor as a lost soul in hell with herself as mother mourning his loss.

There is great potential here for tragic pathos on a grand scale. Curiously enough, however, Salman Rushdie chooses Brechtian distancing devices and deliberate destruction of the fictional illusion, so that we readers are so distanced from the characters that we feel no emotion for them and experience no identification or empathy. Instead readers drown in contrary currents of over-frequent and grandiose appeals to "Edenic heights" or "Judas Christ" or the *Mahabharata* and Troy, alternating with silly pop culture ranging from Popeye to Tonto and John Wayne's westerns. This constant oscillation between parodistic allusions to El Cid or the *Ramayana* on the one hand and the satiric undercutting of this potential pathos by references to Disneyland in the end produces a weariness and an alienated distaste in the reader for Rushdie's posturing characters. The plot becomes a kind of four-ringed circus where the antics of murderous clowns replace a focus on an in-depth evocation of the main characters. What could have been a heart-rending and highly philosophical family saga of decay and defeat in the manner of Thomas Mann's *Buddenbrooks,* becomes instead a posturing, metafictional, postmodernist cross between isolated stories that never become continuous and rather repetitive scholarly glosses by an intrusive author.

This is a great pity because Rushdie is a brilliant storyteller and a great tragic thinker. Isolated passages have great evocative power for the emotions and pyrotechnics of linguistic display. But because Rushdie opts for magic realism and alienation-devices, he perhaps deliberately forgoes the building up of empathy for his central figure, the sad dupe, the Moor. Any forward momentum in the plot is stopped by the detritus of unselective references, images and word-play allusions. This is not so much a novel in which the characters are set free to act and to interact as a collection of scraps of essays constantly commenting on the legends and the anecdotes. Rushdie becomes a latterday Tristram Shandy, an excessively intrusive narrator, whose explanations, mythical guideposts, learned commentary and silly passages from pop culture overwhelm what character development or plot-continuity there might have been.

The Loss of the Golden Age and the Apocalypse of Evil

Half whimsically, Salman Rushdie posits his Golden Age in two different ways and locations. One Golden Age he places in India before the Emergency, in a Goa and a Bombay populated according to Aurora Zogoiby's paintings by multiculturalists: "Jews, Christians, Muslims, Parsis, Sikhs, Buddhists, Jains crowded into her paint-Boabdil's fancy-dress balls and the Sultan [Boabdil] . . . as his old skin dropped from him chrysalis fashion, standing revealed as a glorious butterfly "(227)

The other Golden Age, that of Sultan Boabdil before the fall of the glorious Alhambra, he places in pre-fifteenth century Granada, at the zenith of the Muslim empire in Spain. How ironic, that after years of being under sentence of death by Muslim-fundamentalists, after years of tormented hiding from Muslim-assassins, Salman Rushdie should locate his novel's golden age at the peak of Muslim splendour and present evil as Hindu-fundamentalism in contemporary, post-Emergency Bombay. The Golden Age fell because Sultan Boabdil—reincarnated in this novel as Aurora Zogoiby's son with a club hand, the Moor—did not have the manly courage to defend civilization as represented by the Alhambra.

The Moor in the novel's present fails to defend his mother's honour and fails to preserve her artistic masterpieces. In the novel's *leitmotif* Sultan Boabdil and the Moor (who is really a Christian Jew) are linked for ever: "Well may you weep like a woman . . . for what you could not defend like a man." (432) The Moor fails as tragic hero because he betrays his mother sexually with the sorceress and femme fatale Uma Sarasvati; equally he fails when he joins the thuggish army of Hindu-fundamentalist Mainduck Fielding, who is the main religious enemy of Aurora's multicultural secularism. And at the very end, the Moor fails for a last time, when he lacks the courage to save Aurora's spiritual protagonist, the Japanese woman Aoi Ue, and his face becomes like "the Sultan's face, from which horror, weakness, loss and pain poured like darkness itself, a face in a condition of existential torment reminiscent of Edvard Munch." (218)

And so it is that a work which begins as a family saga with exoticism, action and tragi-comedy in Goa with the da Gama family building a dynasty on the "Black Gold of Malabar" is transformed by horror and evil into a surreal apocalypse of the end of civilization.

But evil in *The Moor's Last Sigh* is not only the evil of Hindu fundamentalism, whose Bombay army is presented with pseudo-comic grotesquerie as teams of cricket-thugs with comic book deformities. Evil is much more the evil within us all. As Moor the narrator sermonizes:

> they are not inhuman, these Mainduck-style little Hitlers, and it is in their humanity that we must locate our collective guilt, humanity's guilt for human beings' misdeeds; for

> if they are just monsters—if it is just a question of King Kong and Godzilla wreaking havoc until the aeroplanes bring them down—then the rest of us are excused. . . . I personally do not wish to be excused. I made my choice and I lived my life. (297)

In *The Moor's Last Sigh* the evil within us all is presented as the vicious gossip, the infidelity that grows out of boredom and squabbling and marital incompatibility, the banal betrayals, the alienating arrogance of artistic genius, the greed for power, the manipulation of others out of a hysterical pleasure in destruction and revenge etc. If this were a novel of psychological realism, it might be construed as a vital weakness that there are four evil villains at work, and they really are the curl the mo villains of pantomime's melodrama. They are: Abraham, the Moor's murderous father and Bombay's arms and drugs crime czar; Mainduck Raman Fielding, the Hindu standover mini-Hitler thug; Uma Sarasvati, the seductive-destructive femme fatale who conspires to destroy her arch-rival in art Aurora by destroying her family; and Vasco Miranda who seeks revenge for a humilating rejection by Aurora because he is seen as a mediocre fraud as an artist and a pretentious clown as a would-be lover.

This is a lot of villains for one novel. But then, this is not a novel of psychological or indeed any other kind of realism. This is fantasy that is bigger than life, characters who grow out of paintings and archetypes, events that are exaggerated and belong to the evil of fairy tales or to a thematic variation of the evil in Shakespeare's great tragedies, *King Lear* (the mad king and the rebellious children), *Othello* (the love-mad Moor), and *Hamlet* (the son fails to avenge his mother's dishonour and murder).

This is a novel which bounds between heaven and hell. The heaven was either in an elusive, multicultural golden age or, briefly, in Aurora's Elephanta. The hell is in the novel's final sequence in a nightmarish sequence of uprootedness, empty commercialism and pointlessness in the allegory of Benengeli.

Mooristan as a Palimpsest-Nightmare of Colliding Realities

Mooristan is the magically heightened twilight-zone. There is a genuine Mooristan that is invented as symbolic territory by master-painter Aurora Zogoiby. But there is also a spurious Mooristan which is the vulgar epigonal imitation of Vasco Miranda in Portugal.

In Aurora's all-important paintings, which determine the narrative structure of this novel, Mooristan is a fusion of Alhambra with the Mughal palace-fortresses in Delhi and Agra. But Mooristan for Aurora is also a palimpsest-nightmare where irreconcilable worlds collide, not only in terms of a surreal, layer-painting technique, but also in terms of revealing hidden worlds of danger and horror lurking beneath superficial surfaces of pseudo-civilization in sex, politics, religion and commerce. This is the central metaphor for *The Moor's Last Sigh*. The palimpsest-image reveals that the benign appearances of our daily reality are only the thinnest of pseudo-veneers stretched over the psycho-frenzy within us all as we are driven by sexual lust, power-lust, bigotry and megalomania.

Universal Conspiracy and the Unknowable Other: The War of All against All

Many of the leading characters attempt to create refuges and retreats where they can withdraw from the hostility of the world and experience security and trust. Camoens da Gama builds two palaces in Goa. Aurora retreats to Elephanta on the cliffs above the Bombay estuary. Mainduck has a fortress guarded by dogs and bodyguards in Bombay. Vasco Miranda constructs his own imitative Elefanta and his tower of silence in the village of the damned. But none of these refuges affords security and peace of mind.

Camoens da Gama is imprisoned by the British for years and emerges a shadow of himself with a stuffed dog on wheels named Jawaharlal. Aurora is allegedly murdered either by her own husband Abraham or by his arch rival Mainduck Fielding.

Abraham is blown up in the thirty-second floor of his elevated garden of Eden by suicide bombers. Mainduck is throttled by the Moor and then blown to smithereens by the same suicide bombers. Vasco murders Aoi Ue in his tower but also experiences his own fatal heroin overdose and bloody death there. There is no security.

Nor is there any trust or loyalty. Aurora allegedly suspects her husband Abraham of wanting to murder her, perhaps in a fit of Othellian jealousy. Mainduck is betrayed and spied on by his own lieutenants. Abraham and Aurora spy on their only son and expel him for alleged betrayal. Aurora spies on her only son's mistress in order to prove that she is promiscuous and manipulative. This mistress Uma in fact tries to murder her besotted lover, the Moor and almost succeeds. Abraham spies on Vasco Miranda in order to have a reason for showing him the door. Yet most of these characters have either been close friends, or possibly lovers, or are family. There is no escape from betrayal. The other remains unknowable and treacherous. Sooner or later all relations end in negation and obsessive hatred. This hatred is far stronger than the love ever was.

The only exception to this universal hatred and murderous violence is the love between the mother-artist Aurora and the son-admirer the Moor. Even after they have both negated their love in one way or another—in sexual betrayal by the Moor and in expulsion and disinheritance of the Moor by his mother—they reaffirm their love. Aurora does this through her final painting of "The Moor's Last Sigh" in which she mourns his descent into hell. The Moor reaffirms his love with his final pilgrimage in search of her stolen paintings which costs him his life. The corpses on stage at the end of this work outnumber even those of Shakespeare's *Hamlet.* But with Salman Rushdie, there remains not even a Fortinbras-witness. The tale is left posthumously as a kind of confession and stations of the cross martyrdom by the dying Moor. With his dying breath, he affirms the transcendental beauty of the Palace of Alhambra in Granada.

Gender-War, Power-Lust and the Fall to Hysteria and Insanity

It is not only the central figure of the Moor who suffers Lucifer's horrendous fall into hell. His mother Aurora suffers the eclipse of her artistic reputation, slander of her moral character, hatred by the Ram-Hindu mobs of her cosmopolitan secularity and her wealth, the burning of most of her masterpieces and possibly murder by the henchman of a spurned suitor. Aurora's fire, energy and artistic vision make her a far more likely candidate for heroic stature than her poor, deformed son who in addition suffers the curse of genes which age him at double the normal rate as yet another way of isolating him from daily forms of average happiness.

The implied, incestuous (but unfulfilled) love between mother Aurora and son Moor give an Oedipal angle to the novel's many accounts of gender-warfare, lust and revenge. Their tortured and mutually betrayed love is nevertheless never destroyed and continues beyond death through Aurora's final masterpiece devoted to the son who she thought had been misled by lust for the treacherous Uma to defile her role as mother. This is why the novel ends with the words of wisdom of the prisoner Aoi Ue to the effect that: "Defeated love is still a treasure, and those who choose lovelessness have won no victory at all." (425)

But apart from this enduring love between heroic mother and duped son, almost all relationships depicted by Rushdie are part of a gender-war which forms an unbridgeable gap between males and females. Even the youthful love of Aurora and Abraham founders on his fear of his mother, his preference for trivial affairs, and her preferencc to devote herself to her painting. Far more horrific than their estrangement, however, is the hysterical conspiracy by the insane Uma to exploit the devoted love of the deformed Moor in order to destroy utterly the entire Zogoiby family. In a sense she is just about successful and only the Moor farcically survives her fiendish attempt to murder him.

The Moor's sister throws herself away on the utterly worthless Johnny Cashondeliveri. And Vasco Miranda suffers daily insults to his art and his person from the woman whom he unsuccessfully adores, Aurora Zogoiby. So, the confusions and disasters of eros are well represented by Salman Rushdie in his accounts of gender-warfare. The Moor's first sister is driven to hysteria and eventually suicide, his other sister takes refuge as a nun in loving a more reliable if somewhat distant Jesus, Uma kills herself unintentionally when she takes the poison pill that she meant for her lover, and Vasco Miranda in his obsessive love-sickness ends up an insane and murderous heroin-addict.

Those characters who aren't driven by unrequited sexual longing are driven by power-lust. This seems to be true equally of the megalomaniacal and criminal rivals for power, the Moor's father Abraham and the Moor's temporary employer Mainduck Fielding. Their power lust does not make them as immediately vulnerable as does the sexual lust of the other characters, but in the end it brings about their fall. There is no security, no stability and no refuge in Rushdie's tormented world.

Historical Background intruding on Subjective Fiction: Faction

There is little doubt that Rushdie means his work to be taken as an allegory of the fall of India, and specifically Bombay, from multicultural tolerance to fanatical sectarianism. The work also seems intended as a lament for the death of the age of heroes and dialogue with the gods and a feeling that we are at the fag-end of history where the leading roles are acted out by clowns and posturers. Specific references to Indian history, some dating back to the Portuguese rule in Goa and the waves of emigration of Jews there over the centuries, ensure that there is a factual background to this strangely surrealistic tale, serving perhaps as an anchor of credibility for the voyages of fantasy and myth on which Rushdie has his much embroidered characters embark.

More covertly, one can feel Rushdie's own tragic, recent history reverberating in the losses and defeats of his protagonist, the half-Jewish "Moor." As the Moor stumbles through webs of erotic deceit, familial treachery and religious-political exploitation, as he descends into the cockroach hell of the Bombay gaol or ascends into the equally cockroach-infested tower prison of the insane Vasco Miranda, as he searches in vain to give and receive love and to belong to someone and somewhere where he can find loyalty and stability, we can feel Salman Rushdie's own fall from world-celebrated author to persecuted pariah in hiding from Islamic death-threats.

The explicit historical background and the implicit autobiographical subtext of a writer who has lost his roots and his sense of belonging combine to give the feeling of "faction" to these otherwise fantastic, farcical and allegorical tales.

The Theology of Agnosticism and the Redemption of Art

Although *The Moor's Last Sigh* is full of religious allusions, these allusions are either parodistic or negative. Aurora's palace to art, the Elefanta, is known as "Edenic heights." Vasco Miranda paints parodies of the crucifixion known as his series on Judas Christ. In one of the Moor's many descents into hell, this time in Bombay prison, Dante is parodied ("Give up such delusive esperance, you rotter" [285]) and the Fall of the devils from heaven ("Scurry along, Beezlebooby! Your After Life awaits" [286]). The fundamentalist Ram-Hinduism of Mainduck Fielding is lampooned as having totally missed the point of the irreducible multiplicity of Hinduism's revelations and gods. Abraham's Biblical sacrifice of his son is referred to, but this is sacriligeous because Abraham in this work is an irreligious criminal.

Nevertheless, this work is filled with religious and spiritual intensity. One of the central, dominating images is that of the tear in the world's surface which can suck unsuspecting victims out of their normal lives and into the vortex of a surreal hell. Heaven may have become a fiction, but hell is more real than ever. Another spiritual image is that of the Moor painfully losing his skin (227), flayed alive in agony, but also beyond despair in the hope of reincarnation to the glory of the Moors in the Alhambra. Or to return like one of world mythology's long-sleepers, King Arthur, Barbarossa, Finn MacCool, the Worm Ouroboros, the Australian Wandjina, and with a deliberate postmodernist anti-climax, Snow White and Rip van Winkle (433)

There is a theology of agnosticism and of blackly humorous egoism in this novel. It culminates in a ludicrous conjunction of Popeye the sailorman with Jehovah: "I yam what I yam an' that's what I yam. . . . God's name turned out to be our own as well. I am, I am, I am. I am. I am. Tell them, I AM hath sent me to you." (433) The same inclination to theological satire and mockery of Islam which got Rushdie into dire straits with *The Satanic Verses* resurfaces here as an irreverent persiflage of Judaism and Christianity.

For a theology of passion in this novel, we must turn to art. Certainly the most passionate and reverent imagery is reserved for the analysis of Aurora's personal mythology on canvas. We read: "Aurora and I posed, somewhat blasphemously, as a godless madonna and child. My stunted hand had become a glowing light, the only light-source in the picture." (220) Quite apart from the blasphemy against Christianity here, there is a determination that if the inadequacies and evil of our selves and our world are to be redeemed, this can only be done by art. Aurora is determined "to transcend and redeem its [the world's] imperfections through art." (220) Similarly, the Moor writes his extended autobiography as a confession of his failures and betrayals and suffering and yearns for redemption by reincarnation in an ultimate work of religious art, the Alhambra.

In fact, *The Moor's Last Sigh* is dominated by the tragic image of the artist. There is Aurora, the tragic seer and theologian of the hellish tear in creation's fabric. There is Vasco Miranda, the clownish and fraudulent artist who suffers the agony of realizing that his art is derivative and mediocre and who gives his life to an agonized and self-defeating revenge which in spite of himself is also a homage to Aurora. Finally, there is the Moor, the artist on pilgrimage from naivety through betrayal and confession to truth and redemption.

From Comic Strip to Tragic Allegory

The Moor's Last Sigh ends where it begins, with the narrator-confessor fleeing from the police across the plains of Spain. His pilgrimage has become a flight after the catastrophe, but it is a flight with a double purpose. The first purpose is to see the Alhambra palace in Granada before he dies. The second purpose is to write and to publicize his confessions as an act of repentance and also of self-justification; like Luther, he says, here I stand, or rather with his customary black humour parody, here I sit in total physical and spiritual exhaustion. His method of distributing his confessions saves a lot in publishing, binding and advertising costs; like a paper-chase for children he leaves a trail of his manuscript-papers behind him, so that his pursuers can learn his life story while they pursue him. This is the justification of life through art as autobiography. The Moor, like his revered murdered mother, says that the horrors of life will be redeemed by art or not at all.

But this is not purist high art. This is postmodernist art full of mixing of the genres, parody, satire, comic book pop culture mixed with allusions to tragic high culture, and a substitution of animated, computer-game super-violence for realistic characters interacting in a credible plot. Nevertheless, it is still meant seriously beyond the jokes as postmodernist art redeeming and celebrating the autobiographical author and his family. Salman Rushdie creates a chaotic, multi-religious world, where the races and the creeds are inter-bred. This postmodernist world tends so to mock the diehard religious sects that still insist that they have the one and only revealed truth, with the result that religious wars become nonsensical and bigotry absurd. Many religions supply the confusing context for archetypal precedents for the characters's deeds, but the truth is that only the tortured creation of art is treated seriously and with passion by the author. Religion can no longer justify life, but true art does.

The Moor is the last of the main characters left. They have all died unnatural, violent deaths and now he too must die an unnatural death because his genes have aged him at twice the normal human rate. This too is presumably to be understood as the mark of Cain on the artist who experiences life with such intensity of emotion and self-torture that he/she ages twice as quickly as bystanders. The Moor's final flight to the Alhambra palace is of course not a flight to the religion of Islam, but a flight for spiritual refuge to a sublime work of art built in an age of Islamic peace, tolerance, scholarship and art as architecture. It is also a flight to identify with his archetypal ancestor, the weak, defeated Sultan Boabdil. Just as Sultan Boabdil had to vacate his Alhambra palace paradise because he was too weak and cowardly to defend it, the Moor has had to lose the paradise of his mother's Elefanta palace of art high above Bombay because he succumbed through blind lust to betrayal of his mother.

So much for the intended structure and meaning of *The Moor's Last Sigh*. When we examine the work from the point of view of narrative method, characterization and mood, however, it becomes apparent that whereas the first two hundred pages could be seen as a farcical family saga, the final two hundred pages are increasingly disjoint and hyperbolic episodes of computer-game violence and mystery incongruously mixed with the serious interpretation of Aurora's paintings as tragic high art.

The poses, antics and cavortings of the family's founders, Camoens da Gama and Aires da Gama and their wives and relatives in the spice mountains of Goa, are related with zest and humour. Narrative distance is maintained. Even the meeting and mating of Portuguese Christian Aurora with Jewish-Indian Abraham are related with zest and humour through the imagery of a peppery consummation in the spice granaries of the port. But by the time their last child, nicknamed the Moor, is born some eighteen years after their increasingly unsuccessful union, the mood of this anti-novel has changed drastically from high good humour to a gloomy enquiry into evil, organized crime, hatred, vicious rumour-mongering, solitude and life as a spiritual sentence to despair. Only Aurora's painting, or the Moor's confessional writing, can protest with integrity against this despair.

Of the siblings in this doomed family, Ina seeks escape in promiscuity in the USA but is laid low by cancer; Minnie seeks refuge as a Christian nun, sees absurd visions of a prophetic rat and dies as Sister Floreas in the armageddon of Bombay's fire-bombing; and Mynah is murdered, probably by her father's henchmen because as a Marxist lawyer she was exposing his organized, commercial crime. So the siblings try all contemporary avenues: mindless pleasure-seeking, Christianity, Marxism, and for the Moor, the despairing confessions of uncommitted, secular art.

But acting as a counterbalance to the chaos, murderous greed, perversion and sectarian bigotry of the world as experienced by the da Gama and then the Zogoiby family, is the narrative method. Narrator-confessor, the club-handed Moor, acts as scholarly art connoisseur and describes and comments on the paintings of his revered mother which interpret and explain this chaos of greed and revenge. Again as a counterbalance to sectarian religious dogma and hatred, the Moor presents himself as a "jewholic-anonymous, a cathjew nut" (16) as the irreligious bastard son of unmarried parents.

The Moor's Last Sigh is a renunciation of institutional religion and a heroisation in spite of postmodernist jokes of the independent, secular artist. It is therefore, indirectly, a justification of Salman Rushdie's own artistic career, as his harsh, satiric vision of the world's sectarian evil earned him powerful enemies ranging from Mrs. Gandhi to the Imams of Islam. Finally, *The Moor's Last Sigh* is a tragic plea from beyond despair for the tolerance of multiculturalism in a world that is rent by ethnic and sectarian hatred and war.

NOTE

1. **Salman Rushdie, *The Moor's Last Sigh* (London: Jonathon Cape, 1995), p. 352.**

A Postmodern, Provocative, Metropolitan Mother India: Aurora Zogoiby of Rushdie's *The Moor's Last Sigh*

P. BALASWAMY

"Nobody ever made a movie called *Father India*" derisively comments the narrator-protagonist, Moreas Zogoiby, in The Moor's Last Sigh, "'Bharat-pita'? Sounds all wrong."[1] What is right, according to Moreas, the 'Moor,' as well as for his creator, Salman Rushdie, is equating one's native land with one's mother, resulting in the image of 'Bharat-mata'/'Mother India.' Elsewhere Rushdie declares: "Motherness . . . is a big idea in India, maybe our biggest: the land as mother, the mother as land, as the firm ground beneath our feet." (137) In his other novels, on the Indian subcontinent also, one can find this concept reiterated, sometimes in a serious vein, but more often in a mocking tone, in tune with his postmodernist ludic sense and irreverence. In Aurora (Da Gama) Zogoiby, the flamboyant mother of the Moor, however, Rushdie goes farther and supplants the traditional image of the kind, compassionate, rural, heroic Mother (courtesy Nargis of Mehboob Khan's classic movie *Mother India*) with, to put it in his own words, his "own sort of Mother India . . . metropolitan, sophisticated, noisy, angry and different."[2] A bitchy, Goan Catholic/Jewess substitutes the kum-kum-clad, devout and divine Hindu female in Rushdie's love/hate novel on India. This paper aims to analyze this "dark, bloody mother India" (5) image splashed throughout this epic novel, with the trappings of his usual, brilliant "chutnification" of contemporary history. It leads us to a vital elevation about Rushdie's art as well as his deep concern for the country of his origin.

Salman Rushdie, the expatriate *enfant terrible* of Indian Writing in English in its postmodern, postcolonial phase, had always been obsessed with a *femme fatale* in each one of his Indian subcontinent trilogy.

Midnight's Children, highly autobiographical, unraveled the horrors felt in the Indian national consciousness due to the travails of the Independence struggle, the Partition of India and the Emergency era. Even though the Saleem Sinai picaresque adventures, "chutnified" with the historical events from 1916 to 1980, were the high spots of the novel, a major part of it was, however, hogged by the 'Madam,' Mrs. Indira Gandhi, the *femme fatale* of the Indian politics and Government in the 60s and 70s. At one end of the spectrum of Mrs. Gandhi's public life was her image as a noble, valiant and idealized/idolized Jhansi ki Rani; and at the other end was perceived an image of the ego-maniacal demoness who devoured her own folks. Rushdie focussed on Saleem Sinai's plight of dispossessedness, impotency and homelessness as a typical condition of the Indian during Mrs. Gandhi's rule. Ironically, even such a *Bhadra Kaali* figure was assigned motherness by Rushdie, despite the terrible nature of her motherhood as perceived by him. Mrs. Gandhi's followers proclaimed that "India was Indira, and Indira was India" during her heydays, a sentiment the Moor echoes in *The Last Sigh*, when he describes Indira-Mata as "the living mother-goddess of us all." (137)

No less devastating is the *femme fatale* of his second historiographic metafiction *Shame*, Sufia Zinobia, the personification of shame visited upon this subcontinent when partition between India and Pakistan was effected. Another devouring monster, Sufia is the feminine embodiment of the nightmare that millions of people went through in Pakistan and India. The horror of Sufia was emphasized by Rushdie in his pointed references to the unmotherly, unfeminine and irrational deeds indulged in by her in her metamorphosed state.

The Moor's Last Sigh, the last of the triptych, an allegory of India in the 90s, has the surface structure of the Zogoiby-Da

Gama saga stretching from 1990 to 1993. Briefly stated, the novel traces the Jewish and Goan-Christian ancestry of Abraham Zogoiby, a billionaire Bombayite and his famed artist-wife, Aurora (Da Gama) Zogoiby, and their rise to fame and riches from the pepper estate of Cochin to their fabulous Malabar Hill residence and the Zogoiby enterprises—'Ziodi Corporation'—the third richest of Indian enterprises. A multi-layered epic novel which performs with astonishing brilliance at various levels, it paints (no other imagery will suit this scorching tale of a painter protagonist) (1) the Oedipal mix-up involving Aurora Zogoiby, her son Moreas ('Moor') Zogoiby and his mistress Uma Sarasvati!; (2) the underworld operations of the Big Business Houses in Bombay and their devastating gang wars; (3) the alarming rise to power of the Hindu, Muslim fundamentalist groups, their fanning of communal fires [one cannot resist the temptation to mention their current ire over the movie *Fire*!] and its impact on the Indian society, economics, politics, arts, sports and other invisible spheres all over the country, especially in Bombay. Breathtaking in its multivalent dimensions, *The Moor's Last Sigh* is the 'sigh' of a non-Hindu about the catastrophic Ayodhya events and their poisonous aftermath. Instead of adopting a polar opposite viewpoint of a Muslim victim, the novel objectifies the suicidal track chosen by our nation, through a Jew victim/victimizer's point of view, not sectarian anyhow, but with a pluralistic and multicultural ethos.

In the India of the last four decades, in its pluralistic, modern malleable, multilingual and multicultural phases, the *idee fixe* about Mother India has to undergo a radical change. Rushdie catches on this need for a revolutionary revision of a commonly accepted opinion by presenting the fiery and flamboyant Aurora Zogoiby as the typical Mother India. What a yawning contrast she is to the image fostered by Nargis in the Fifties! In a true postmodernist fashion, Rushdie provides blaring references to his readers to start this comparison game, not the subtle, mild hints of the traditional storytellers. In fact, the narrator and the other characters lead the readers to this critical practice. The Moor comments:

> The year I was born, Mehboob Productions' all-conquering movie *Mother India*—three years in the making, three hundred shooting days, in the top three all-time mega-grossing Bollywood flicks—hit the nation's screens. Nobody who saw it ever forgot that glutinous saga of peasant heroinism, that super-slushy ode to the uncrushability of village India made by the most cynical urbanites in the world. And as for its leading lady—O Nargis with your shovel over your shoulder and your strand of black hair tumbling forward over your brow!—she became, until Indira-Mata supplanted her, the living mother-goddess of us all. (137)

A fictional stormy meeting between the real-life Nargis Dutt and imaginary Aurora Zogoiby takes place on the semi-realistic terrace of the Malabar Hill palace, *Elephanta*, in which, a legendary, sacred mother-son relationship is demolished by the rambunctious, wildly funny narrator/author. The remarkable passage provides a vital clue to our argument: "In *Mother India*, a piece of Hindu myth-making directed by a Muslim socialist, Mehboob Khan, the Indian peasant woman is idealized as bride, mother, and producer of sons; as long-suffering, stoical, loving, redemptive and conservatively wedded to the maintenance of the social status quo." (138-39)

There can be no doubt about this image of the 'Bharat Nari,' fostered for ages by writers, artists and our popular media. *Manusmriti* had codified it, the great Indian epics, the *Ramayana* and the *Mahabharata* have shown ideal figures of women in Sita, Savitri et al in glorious light, and our popular media have nourished this image over the decades. Some positive features of this image notwithstanding, this patriarchal concept, oppressive and imprisoning, is getting to be increasingly objected to and rejected by the modern Indian females.

Indian society, in its globalization, MNC phase, seeds of which were sown in the Fifties themselves, has witnessed far-reaching changes being effected not only in its social and economic spheres, but in the psychological, cultural ethical makeup of the individuals, too. The changes are more daringly and glaringly adopted among the Indian women in their outlook, behaviour and attitude. The 'Bharat Nari' image, in particular, has received many severe beatings, the ramifications of which are yet to be felt on a large scale.

Rushdie, a novelist with his sharply sensitive antenna, also perhaps the physical distance he has to keep from the Indian society making his vision clear in its contours, unerringly captures these sea-changes in the Indian woman's psyche. The British-fed and expatriate Bombayite he is, some kind of westernization 'Westoxication' as he would like to call it (178)] in his conceptualization and execution process is rather inevitable. Despite such minor aberrations, Rushdie is not wide of the mark in his portrayal of a metropolitan and provocative Mother India in Aurora Zogoiby. As his protagonist put it rather brutally, it is "an image of an aggressive, treacherous, annihilating mother who haunts the fantasy life of Indian males." (139)

Reverting back to the traits mentioned earlier, of a traditional Mother India, one can find that Rushdie's story systematically breaks that image when it provides the characteristics of this radical, urban Mother India. Aurora Da Gama, from her girlhood, proves herself to be a ruthless, exploitative, calculative and even cruel female. Aurora's mother Isabella had run a cold war with her mother-in-law, Epifania, from the moment Cameons chose to marry, in the old lady's opinion, a "hussy from somewhere." (23) Isabella's only child Aurora also harbours a deep hatred and ill-will towards her grandmother. Her reactions to Epifania's last, dying moments on the chapel floor on Christmas eve of 1938 are so cold and calculated that these would have horrified any other family member present there. Epifania is struck by a fatal paralysis as she is praying alone in the chapel into which accidentally Aurora, the sixteen-year-old girl looking for some diversion from her monthly pains, peeps. Quickly grasping the situation, the young one sits down on the floor, cross-legged and watches on, not even lifting her finger to help the suffering old lady. It is a cold-blooded murder, if one admits that murder can be committed by inaction. A chilling scene (62-64) that shows Aurora to be some kind of demoness, equalled in horror only by Sufia Zinobia in her tearing moments.

Nargis's Mother India is a coy mistress, an ideal bride, subdued and subjected, a true 'Bharat Nari' on her nuptial night. Aurora Da Gama's "marriage" with Abraham Zogoiby, in contrast, is a public scandal, since the girl is just fifteen, fresh and innocent, and Abraham is her father's age—thirty-five. Add to that the fact that Aurora is the rich Christian heiress and Abraham is a poor, inconsequential Jewish employee of her father's spices' company. Accidentally meeting him in a pepper godown, Aurora instantly falls in love with the handsome Jew, draws him "by the chin" literally and fornicates with him then and there high up on pepper sacks stacked up to the godown roof. (88-90) She even defies her Uncle Aires and he deserts his old mother Flory, to the chagrin of the elders, all for the sake of their mad, "pepper love." In true Shylock fashion, she demands that he become a Christian in order to marry her. Aurora is thus "a shameless hussy," as her grandmother would put it, in going through her stormy marriage with a scandal to boot at every stage—in stark contrast to the soft demure bride of tradition who marries a man even without looking at his face.

One aspect of the conventional bride/wife, celebrated in literature and movies, is her steadfast love, devotion and fidelity to her husband. The heroine of *Mother India* demonstrates these qualities in an admirably slushy manner. Aurora's score on these counts is not only dismal, but scandalous, too. Her love for Abraham evaporates after a few years of conjugal life, especially when she learns that Abraham has started fooling around with girls during her absences. She pays him back in his own coin—by launching her own extra-marital affairs: one of them, the Moor audaciously reports, is with the first Prime Minister of India—Jawaharlal Nehru. In fact, the boy Moreas strongly suspects that Nehru might have sired him. (176-77) Uma, the Moor's mistress, accuses that Aurora had three affairs, which every Bombayite knew, with "that retard Kekoo Mody," "Vasco Miranda, the fat fraud," and "*Mainduck* Raman Fielding." (256) Quite strangely, Abraham, perhaps out of a guilty conscience, never acts the role of a righteously angry husband, allowing and suffering her indiscretions silently, all because of his love for her: "The greater, the more public her betrayals, the more overwhelming, and secret, grew his love." (170) This "bitchy, cosmopolitan, Westoxicated" Aurora Zogoiby is the Moor's concept of metropolitan Mother India!

If *Mother India* projected an ideal mother as "producer of sons," (139) the Moor's Mother India begets three daughters—Christina, Inamorata and Philomena—and one son, Moreas; of these four children, only one survives. Aurora outlives her children and, in a sense, contributing to, at least two deaths. In a prophetic statement much earlier in the story, she proclaims: "We all eat children . . . If not other people's, then our own." (125) Reputed for her "legendary stubbornness [and] determination," (125) she refuses to breast feed her daughters and agrees to do it for the Moor, as he is an abnormal child.

The fact that the Moor is "the only child she suckled at her breast" (129) has Freudian implications, overtly and covertly scattered throughout the novel, and also in the movie *Mother India*, as well as in the lives of its stars. Fascinating and intricate weaving of the elements of real and imaginary lives—both on screen and off, and in the novel—has been handled in a masterly manner by Rushdie. That Nargis (who played the role of the mother in *Mother India*) married Sunil Dutt (who played the bad son's role) in real life is everybody's knowledge; but transforming this Oedipal element into the celluloid story, by finding a couple of apt references in the naming process in the movie, has been a masterly stroke of Rushdie.

The mischievous mix up between fiction and real life is worth quoting in full. Aurora has invited Nargis and Sunil Dutt to her Malabar Hill residence:

> "The first time I saw that picture," she confided to the famous movie star on the high terrace at *Elephanta*, "I took one look at your Bad Son, Birju, and I thought, O boy, what a handsome guy. . . . And now look—you have gone and marry-o'ed him! What sexy lives you

> movie people leadofy *to marry your own son*, I swear, wowie." (my italics)

When Sunil Dutt tries to explain that she is mixing up fact and fancy, life and movie, Aurora persists:

> Even in the picture, . . . I knew right off that bad Birju had the hots for his gorgeous ma.
>
> Nargis stood speechless, open-mouthed. Vasco Miranda, who could never resist a bit of trouble-making, saw the storm brewing and made haste to join in. "Sublimation," he offered, "of mutual parent-child longings, is deep-rooted in the national psyche. The use of names in the picture makes the meaning clear. This 'Birju' moniker is also used by God Krishna, isn't it, and we know that milky 'Radha' is the blue chap's one true love. In the picture, Sunil, you are made up to look like the god, and you even fool with all the girls, throwing your stones to break their womby water-pots; which, admit it, is Krishna-esque behaviour. In this interpretation," and here clowning Vasco attempted unsuccessfully to convey a certain scholarly *gravitas*, "*Mother India* is the dark side of the Radha-Krishna story, with the subsidiary theme of forbidden love added on. But what the hell, Oedipus-schmeoedipus! Have another chotta peg." (138)

In her remarks here, the daring Aurora seems to express a hidden longing for her own handsome, hefty son Moreas. [Owing to a freakish genetic factor, the Moor grows faster than normal children. By age ten, he had grown into a full-fledged adult of great proportions. His big sister Ina comments: "You have become Mr. Gulliver-Travel and we are your Lilliputs." (188)] This Oedipal element has been dormant in her probably from the day she suckled her only son. One way of sublimating her original sexual impulse is seen in her artistic endeavours, which result in the famous 'Moor paintings.' In two of her sketches, the Oedipal element is revealed, though in a reversed manner. In the first picture, Aurora paints "herself as the young Eleanor Marx and me as her father Karl. *Moor and Tussy* was a rather shocking idea—my mother girlish, adoring, and I in patriarchal, lapel-gripping pose, . . . 'If you were twice as old as you look, and I was half as old as I am, I could be your daughter,' my forty-plus mother explained." (224) The second painting *To Die upon a Kiss* is more revealing of the hidden impulses: she portrayed herself as murdered Desdemona and son Moreas as Othello! (224-25) Shocking though these Freudian explications are, Rushdie seems to be more amused at the parallels with *Mother India* movie's stars proving the point in an ironic life-imitates-art fashion.

Not only is Rushdie's Mother India figure the antithesis of the popular image in her roles as bride, wife and mother, Aurora is never "redemptive" nor "conservatively wedded to the maintenance of the social status-quo"; on the other hand, she is a sharply-retaliating, vindictive woman in many of her reactions. Once again Rushdie is particular in portraying the modern Indian woman as not tolerant anymore (of her husband's sins, for example), retaliatory and furious. Gone is the tendency to treat the husband with reverential acceptance even if he were to be metaphorically "a stone or a blade of grass." When Aurora learns that her husband had agreed to give up their first born to his angry and demanding mother Flory, she simply shuts him out of her bed room and vows not to indulge in conjugal love as long as her mother-in-law is alive. (114-15) To spite her mother-in-law's effort to snatch her first born, Aurora launches herself on the national scene.

Rushdie has often resorted to a device in his earlier novels, too, of linking the personal life of his protagonist with the historically famous events, for it is one technique which he employs to burlesque history. A critic has observed: "Narrative never follows the emotional logic of the characters' lives, but the brittle, externally determined contours of 'current events.' Rushdie deliberately prevents his readers from being caught up in a story with its own 'organic' life, that progresses uninterrupted, and that creates a completely imagined world."[3] Thus we find that Rushdie presents an amusing mixture of the personal perversities of his protagonist with her glorious public career/life as part of the Independence struggle:

> Aurora Zogoiby grew into the giant public figure we all know, the great beauty at the heart of the nationalist movement, the loose-haired bohemian marching badly alongside Vallabhai Patel and Abdul Kalam Azad when they took out processions, the confidante—and according to persistent rumours, mistress—of Pandit Nehru, his 'friend of friends,' who would later vie with Edwina Mountbatten for his heart. Distrusted by Gandhiji, loathed by Indira Gandhi, her arrest after the Quit India resolution of 1942 made her a national heroine. . . . People began saying that Aurora Zogoiby was the new Chand Bibi, standing up against a different and even more powerful Empire. (116)

A brilliant instance of Rushdie's 'chutnification' of history, this parodic exercise of turning gossip into history serves a vital function for the creator. It is a stroke of genius to refashion "Mother India as a bitch-goddess." As Rukmini Bhaya Nair has pointed out, "It creates exactly that ironic gap for post-Rushdie postcoloniality to manifest itself—the gap between the stodgy, unidimensional portrait of a traditional Mother India beloved of the early days of Nehruvian nationalism and the multivalent image of a mother whose wandering sons are as unpredictable and ambiguous as herself." (XII)

The *Bharat Nari* portrait Rushdie presents in *The Moor's Last Sigh* has yet another dimension in the character of Uma Sarasvati, his love, who is supposed to look like his mother, Aurora. Rushdie's penchant for stealing contemporary personalities for making them figures of his fiction reaches its most controversial point in his turning Bal Thackeray, the maverick Shiv Sena leader of Bombay, and Uma Bharati, another irrepressible leader of a political party wedded to Hindu fundamentalism, as Raman Fielding and Uma Sarasvati, respectively, in his novel. In Uma Sarasvati, the enigmatic Mata Hari, for whom the Moor develops a grand and tragic passion which leads to his fall, Rushdie paints a radical whose commitment to her cause matches her histrionic and chameleon talents to maintain an incredibly deceptive facade. Convinced that the Muslims, the Christians and other minority communities are harming the interests of the majority community of Hindus, Uma Sarasvati plots to destroy the Moor, the only male heir of the fabulously rich Jew. But, a ludicrous, last minute farce, a slapstick clash of heads reverse their roles, and consequently, their fates, whereby she ends up as the dead. The predator that Uma is, she makes terrible unimaginable use of Moor's passion for her to poison his parents's minds against him. The Moor's final evaluation of Uma is striking: "I imagined a chameleon-like creature, a cold-blooded lizard from across the cosmos, who could take human form, male or female, as required, for the express purpose of making as much trouble as possible. . . . Turbulence, disruption, misery, catastrophe, grief—all these were on the menu of its preferred foods." (320)

The advent of persons like Uma Sarasvati on the Indian political scene forebodes a disastrous phase, not only for the Indian polity, but for its society too, which had practised pluralism in an exemplary manner all along. "Turbulence, disruption, catastrophe, grief" are the outcome of the actions/reactions of Uma Sarasvati/Raman Fielding group's activities and attitudes, as well as the underground workings of the mafia men like Scar (a Muslim fanatic) or even Abraham Zogoiby. One evil does not justify another evil—the theses of *The Moor's Last Sigh* emphasizes this age-old maxim. What is quite intriguing, according to Rushdie's portrayal of the tragic events of Ayodhya and its aftermath, is that the traditionally marginalized, oppressed women of India might have a key role to play in the new Indian society that is emerging at the end of the millennium.

The emergence of a fiery substitute for the traditional image of Mother India in the character of Aurora Zogoiby is accomplished in a truly postmodern mingling of Roman, Zudiac-Christian and Hindu myths of goddess of dawn/gardens, is hinted at—"Paradise of Aurora." This classical Paradise is turned into Biblical Heaven, the seat of God Almighty, when Vasco Miranda compares the Moor to Lucifer "hurled from that fabulous garden and plunged towards Pandemonium." (5) The point, however, is stressed that this Edenic paradise contains in itself an "infernal private universe." (5) Aurora, in another context, is "a godless madonna" in her own painting. (220) The madonna being a metropolitan dame, unhesitating in passing a severe sentence on her own offspring for his evil deed, metamorphoses into a "monster": "O, an age of monsters is come upon us. Kalyug, when cross-eyed red-tongued Kali, our mad dam, moves among us wreaking havoc." (228) The mythic references, however, have a contradictory portent in typical postmodernist spirit.

Rushdie's iconoclastic exercise, its satiric and cynical tone and tenor notwithstanding, reveals his deep concern about the catastrophic path chosen by the country of his origin in recent times. In Rushdie's reckoning, the image of Mother India as a "bitch goddess" projected through the two female protagonists of this novel calls for a deep and sustained introspection. Following the footsteps of his literary ancestors, Jonathan Swift and Alexander Pope, he has drawn a bitter and scorching painting of the country which he has left, but cannot forget, and which has deserted him under various compulsions. [One may add here that he had indulged in similar satiric exercises earlier in his second and third novels, too.] This way leads you to disaster, he seems to be warning Indians, if Aurora Zogoiby is the kind of mother that modern India nurtures. Though he zoomed upon the nihilistic aspects quite often, Rushdie, being a true artist with a passion for the truth, admits the greatness of the nation amidst this gloom. Aurora's paintings, often used as metaphors and commentaries of/on reality, show that there is yet a saving grace available in the nation's plurality: "that exploration of an alternative vision of India-as-mother, not Nargis's sentimental village-mother, but a mother of cities, as heartless and lovable, brilliant and dark, multiple and lonely, mesmeric and repugnant, pregnant and empty, truthful and deceitful." (204)

One of the characters in Benengeli village in Spain (where Vasco Miranda had fled to with Aurora's 'Moor' painting) utters the following words to Vasco: "Men and women who leave their natural places are less than human. Either something is lacking in their souls or else something surplus has gotten inside—some manner of devil seed." (327) One may view this comment as the tragic, self-deprecatory words of Rushdie himself, who has been under the double fate of expatriation and a *fatwa*. It seems to indicate the "twice-doomed" [in contrast to the "twice-born" status that he should enjoy] condition of Rushdie. Whatever factors drove a person out of his native land, his love for his mother country will surface quite often, despite the hostile poses he may adopt. Rushdie's art is allegorical in its most sophisticated garb, very effectively hiding his motives. *The Moor's Last Sigh* is yet another demonstration of his love for India under the guise of a parodical allegory.

NOTES

1. Salman Rushdie, *The Moor's Last Sigh* (London: Vintage, 1996), p. 168.
2. Rukmini Bhaya Nair, "What did Rushdie Mean and Why?" *The Hindu*, Literary Review, August 17, 1997, p. xii.
3. Timothy Brennan, *Salman Rushdie and the Third World: Myths of the Nation* (London: Macmillan, 1989), pp. 84-85.

Salman Rushdie's *The Moor's Last Sigh*: Creativity and Controversy

PRADEEP TRIKHA

Salman Rushdie's sixth novel *The Moor's Last Sigh* has upset a lot of people. It has inflamed both enthusiasm as well as resistance, of course not with the same intensity as his *The Satanic Verses* did. As one of the critics points out, the parallel between the two "only brings out the old rivalry between reality managers and the outcasts from the programmed reality."[1] Both in *The Moor's Last Sigh* and *The Satanic Verses* are words of the writer which have electrified the society in the same fashion as the words of "reality managers" like Khomeini and Thackeray. But little did they realize that writers like Rushdie, in their endeavour to deconstruct the society they live in, are the life-blood of some finest writing today. Gunter Grass's *The Call of the Toad*, a depiction of the post-war disenchantment and march of the neo-Nazi also faced ban in Germany. Marques in his *One Hundred Years of Solitude* like Grass and Rushdie tries to redeem contemporary man and makes sense of a cruel history. But unlike them he does not face ban.

Recently, Taslima Nasreen's *Lajja* also paid for its belief in life; Mani Ratnam for his film "Bombay" faced bans and detestation; all these cases have one thing in common and that is BAN which is an expression of impotency of the banning authority. It would be better to remember creative artists, writers and film makers for their creativity and not controversy.

The Moor's Last Sigh spins around the saga of a Jewish Christian family of multiple stock with mixed heritages. It is a dazzling mix of satire and sadness, history and humour. The novel is set against the back-drop of contemporary India. Rushdie gives an expression to his prolonged despair over fast deteriorating social edifice, everything is in mayhem and total anarchy. The historicity and contemporaneity in multi-layers of meanings add motif to the novel.

As far as major themes are concerned, one of course is miscegenation and the other rootlessness—both have their origin and culmination in the Moor's plight. Rushdie's characters are of two kinds: main characters and the point of view characters, both are interdependent and have a sort of organic unity. In one of his interviews, Rushdie says that the book communicates "a sense of urgency." The narrator is "running out of time, living too fast."[2] This justifies his use of the method of layering, truth being concealed under the matters as the life is in the present-day world.

The ban is a curb on the freedom of expression, a censorship on satire but it has failed to make any dent in Rushdie's creativity and sensitive perception of the world he lives in. As he himself said in a seminar on Writers against the State: "One of the things a writer is for is to say the unsayable, to speak the unspeakable, to ask difficult questions. Everybody has answers. Answers are cheap. Questions are hard to find. If you ask those questions that is a proper function of the writer." Rushdie seems to be an angry man and his anger culminates in *The Moor's Last Sigh* which has deafening effect.

II

The Moor's Last Sigh is the story of a life-force, a destiny, a logic, that shows Bombay in its "present state of criminalization and communal disrepair."[3] Rushdie reassembles the story of Moraes Zogoiby from historical bits and pieces which he gathers from Malabar coast to Malabar hill, from Bombay to Benengeli. Moraes says:

> Mine is the story of the fall from grace of a high-born cross-breed: me Moraes Zogoiby, called 'Moor,' for most of my life the only male heir to the spice-trade-'n'-big-

> business crores of the da Gama-Zogoiby dynasty of Cochin, and of my banishment from what I had every right to think of as my natural life by my mother Aurora, nee da Gama, most illustrious of our modern artists, a great beauty who was also the most sharp-tongued woman of her generation 'handing' out the hot stuff to anybody who came within range. (5)

Maternally, he belongs to the generation of Vasco da Gama. His great grandfather, Francisco da Gama, in 1916 joined the Home Rule campaign of Annie Besant and Bal Gangadhar Tilak, and in prison propounded a theory on "The Transformational Fields of Conscience," in which he proposed that each man has spiritual energy similar to electro-magnetic fields. The theory was extensively criticized. Moraes's grandfather remained obsessed throughout his life with the Bolshevik Revolution so much so that he would adopt the leader's image to local needs. His brother was a closet homosexual who named his bull dog as Jawahar Lal, as a protest against imperial loyalty.[4] Moraes's father Abraham Zogoiby deals in underworld activities like trading of girls, explosives and drugs. And with him Rushdie introduces contemporary Bombay full of sound and fury.

A significant role is played by the women in the novel. The great grandmother Epifania, a dominating personality who lived during 1877-1938, fails in her endeavour to hold the reins of family business after her husband's death. She hands over her business to her younger daughter-in-law Carmen da Gama. Epifania triggered family feud and da Gama business empire disintegrated. Moraes's mother Aurora da Gama's marriage could never get approval from Epifania but Aurora with overwhelming presence kills her: "Aurora reached the top . . . saw that 'the Chapel doors were open. . . . [She] . . . crept forward, peered in. . . . Just then, in complete silence Epifania Menzes da Gama fell sideways and lay still. 'One day you will killofy my heart' . . . that death had been swift and merciful." (63)

Epifania throughout her life felt that she was wronged by her husband and grandson Abraham because they could not give her due respect. Her discontentment with life comes in the form of apocalyptic prophecies before her death. "The concept of 'motherness' is looked at from a new perspective. Moraes introspects Motherness. 'Excuse me if I underline the point—is a big idea in India, maybe our biggest: the land as mother, the mother as land, the firm ground beneath our feet.'" (137) This ironical introspection comes to Moraes on looking at his relatives with Aurora who give him the burden of miscegenation, burden of curses, and uncertainty, though Rushdie feels that mother-son relationship in a metropolitan city is drastically different from a heroic peasant woman image of Mother India. Thus he creates his sort of metropolitan Mother India who could offer nothing but rootlessness to her own son: "Nine months to the day before I arrived, there was a missing night. But innocent-till-proven-otherwise is an excellent rule. Jawaharlal Nehru was sixty seven years old in 1957, my mother was thirty two. They never met again." (177-78)

Uncertainty prevails from the moment of his conception to his birth; his birth has been spectacular, as well as his growth. He among his family members was like a Gulliver who falls headlong into a purgatory authored for him by all those who claimed to have some role in his 'gasping life.'

Moraes, rejected by his mother, goes into exile. He echoes his creator's sadness of exile. Like Rushdie, Moraes is "as if cast out from paradise. . . . Displacement was a way for [him] to experience another reality. Another reason is that he should not just stay in the high rise world" but also move in the darker world.[5]

Moor's plight is that he experiences rootlessness and alienation in the society because of its fast-changing value system which he is unable to accept, thinks himself to be out of place and out of time. Moraes grows up in a pluralistic society in which his mother paves her way to national glory and his father Abraham Zogoiby becomes most influential business tycoon. He also investigates in lives of a gallery of rogues: Raman Fielding, an ex-cartoonist, better known as Mainduck, is a leader of regional communal party Mumbai Axis (MA) and has ambitious plans to convert India into a Hindu Rashtra. He conquers the people with his fiery speeches.

It is here in the book that we perceive Rushdie's brilliance to have etched a caricature that many believe to be of Shiv Sena Chief Bal Thackeray, which provoked the leader to give his verdict to restrain the book to enter his domain—Bombay.

Thus, Rushdie not only ridicules the India that Nehru brought into being but actually laments the damage done to the vision in the succeeding years. He zooms in on the apocalyptic days: the post-Ayodhya Bombay bomb blasts, India's capacity to consume the news of Rajiv Gandhi's assassination and feels that life in the metropolis is beyond repair as it is controlled by the underworld dons and white clad politicians, sometimes in nexus with each other and at times in rivalry. In contrast to all this, Rushdie also mentions that Miss India becomes Miss World—becomes the Helen of Troy of the Bombay dons who spread their tentacles around her.

III

Aurora Zogoiby, Moor's mother, deals with the literal palimpsests. Her paintings reveal spirit of the age, intense passion and sacrifice. She also paints the vilest of Bombay's villains, as another painting is painted by her protege-turned inquisitor—Vasco Miranda that conceals her image. It is interesting to notice that Moraes undertakes a long journey from Bombay to Benengeli in Spain in search of the mysterious missing portrait of his mother. The painting has autobiographical element of Rushdie's real life. As he tells L.K. Sharma, "Krishen Khanna, the painter told me that when he was very young some 50 years ago, he painted my mother's portrait and my father refused to buy it. I think he thought it was too sensual. Khanna left it in M.F. Hussain's Studio. And at some point Hussain painted another picture on top of my mother's portrait and that painting was sold. . . . The image of that last painting has stayed. . . There is no other sense in which Aurora is my mother."[6] The missing painting has fitted into the texture of the novel's theme of layered reality; it acts like an inspiring palimpsest. Rushdie also considers that Bombay offers palimpsest life to the people: "The city itself, perhaps the whole country, was a palimpsest, Under World beneath Over World, black market beneath white when the whole life was like this, when an invisible reality moved phantomrise beneath a visible fiction, subverting all its meanings. . . . How could any of us have escaped that deadly layering? . . . How could we have failed to be grotesque?" (184-85) The motif of palimpsest plays an important role in Moor's life especially when his love's labour is lost in his affairs with Uma Saraswati and Nadia Wadia. It also indicates the writer's lament about the pointlessness of art in the face of the invisible reality subverting all its meanings. Sanjay Iyer says: "Love is one of the greatest victims of this subversion of meanings." Rushdie explores the outer world of his characters. This provides "great compression and intensity," as he has a large canvas, a large cast of characters and a large number of incidents, thus "the idea of layering, in the world hidden underneath other worlds" acts as the method of writing the novel.

IV

The blurb on the inner flap of the book claims: "Surpassing even the imaginative brilliance of *Midnight's Children*, *The Moor's Last Sigh* is spectacularly ambitious, funny. Satirical and compassionate. It is a love song to a vanishing world, but also its last hurrah." Rushdie has travelled a long way from his *Midnight's Children* as far as his imagination is concerned; he has also attained maturity and brilliance which makes *The Moor's Last Sigh* "spectacularly ambitious." Another remarkable feature is that it testifies his "imaginative brilliance" because no other writer has ever thought of reconstructing a family saga of four generations in a compact manner. If on one hand like Marquez in *One Hundred Years of Solitude*, Rushdie draws on life and times of generations of a family, on the other hand unlike him he does not refer to the solitude of generations but introduces a wide range of exciting, thrilling and gasping solution related to the

Moor's "extensive travelling, maternal curses, the epidemic love and betrayals, of rites and passions and dance of death?" The saga revolves around the cross breed of a Jewish Christian family. L.K. Sharma significantly points out that the narrator cherishes his inheritance and introduces himself as someone who is neither a Catholic nor a Jew, both or nothing. Below this lies another story of India's reality which is "so plural and so shifting." Rushdie focusses on identity markers like caste, religion, language or place or community, though, now these roots have been uprooted and call in for redefinition.

Rushdie believes that satire is the soul of good literature. The book has several rib-tickling passages revealing spoonerism and malapropism. He has peppered his prose with Hindi words metaphorically: the comptrollers in a Kerala spice company are called Mr. Elaichipillai Kalonjee, Mr. V.S. Mirchandalchini and Mr. Karipattam Tejpattam.[6] Then there is a pseudo-Bharat Goddess (Mother India) called Aurora. Rushdie spares no opportunity to expose linguistic snobbery often seen among educated Indians to prove their superiority over their fellow countrymen.

Thus, *The Moor's Last Sigh* is a satirical criticism of life which is a worthwhile creative endeavour. The State or any political leader has no right to infringe on the right to freedom of expression. Instead they should give Rushdie a 'poetic licence' to think on his line of argument and express something which should be viewed critically and objectively rather than subjectively. What though even if it raises a bit of controversy?

NOTES

1. S. Prasannarajan, "Who's Afraid of Rushdie?" *The Indian Express*, 23 Aug. 1995, p. 6.
2. L.K. Sharma, "To Feel Exiled by India is a Harsh Thing for Me," An Interview, *The Times of India*, New Delhi, Sept. 9, 1995, p. 14.
3. Sanjay Iyer, "The Palimpsest of Life," *Indian Review of Books*, Vol. V, No. 1, pp. 68-69.

4. Amrit Dhillon, "I am Pessimistic about the Changes Occurring in India: An Interview," *India Today*, Sept. 30, 1995, pp. 100-5. Rushdie clarifies, "This is not a novel that sets out to ridicule India that Nehru brought into being, but actually to lament the damage done to the vision of India in the succeeding years. . . . Most leading characters are in favour of independence except one . . . who in order to annoy his family names his dog Jawahar Lal.
5. S. Prasannarajan, "The Last Salaam," *The Indian Express*, Magazine, 20 Aug. 1995, p. 1.
6. P. Lal, "Salman the Magnificient," *Indian Book Chronicle*, Vol. XX, Nos. 10 & 11, Oct.-Nov. 1995, pp. 5-8.

Jhumpa Lahiri's *Interpreter of Maladies*: A Study

A.K. MUKHERJEE

Jhumpa Lahiri's *Interpreter of Maladies*, a collection of nine stories, a maiden venture, has bagged Pulitzer prize for fiction 2000. It is a great honour for an Indian writer writing in English. This is another milestone after Arundhati Roy's *The God of Small Things*. Indian fiction in English from Raja Rao to Jhumpa Lahiri is a long road—arduous, but exciting and exhilarating. Its expansion is both vertical and horizontal. The present paper makes an attempt to study the nine stories of Jhumpa Lahiri, both in its content and form.

Jhumpa Lahiri is different from other Indian writers writing in English. Most of the Indian fiction writers writing in English are born and brought up in India, although the writers like Anita Desai, Kamala Markandaya, Jhabvala, Vikram Seth, Salman Rushdie are living either in England or America. Lahiri was born in London, of Bengali parents, grew up in Rhode Island, U.S.A. Naturally, her connection with India may be through her parents and grandparents. So her knowledge of India is bound to be confined to the stories from her grandparents, parents, books and newspapers. India would appear to her sometimes full of wonders, sometimes full of beggars. But the writers who live outside India and confidently write or comment on the economic, social, political and religious scenario may appear very often exaggerating or under-rating. They are liable to lack honesty and authenticity, which a writer should possess. From this standpoint, Jhumpa Lahiri is honest and authentic to her experiences. She writes about the Indians who have settled either in the USA or

England and does not comment on something that she is not well-versed in. The Indians who have settled abroad feel themselves exiled, as they are in their consciousness unable to cut off completely their umbilical chords that still bind them in their emotional crisis.

Interpreter of Maladies is called "Stories of Bengal, Boston and Beyond." The first story of the book, "A Temporary Matter," relates to the life of Sukumar and Shobha in Boston. The temporary matter is that their electricity would be cut off for an hour for five days. The story is confined to those five days when there will be no electricity for an hour. During those five days Sukumar and Shobha come closer after the day's busy schedules; in the darkness they play games like telling each one a story from his or her own life. Sukumar welcomed this power cut for an hour as darkness could bring them closer despite differences submerged in their relationship. In darkness they could speak out their minds to each other. The past, however bitter it may be, looks romantic and beautiful when viewed through the window of the present. But in the morning of the fifth night, the electric company announced that there would be no power cut on that evening as the line had been repaired ahead of its scheduled time. It disappointed Sukumar. But he kept the room dark from eight p.m., and waited for the game. After their dinner Shobha switched on the light and announced, "I've been looking for an apartment and I've found one." (21) They had enough of enough. Now she needed some time alone. It shocked Sukumar. He thought of telling her the secret he had kept from her. The secret was that she had given birth to a dead male child which he had kept from her as it might have shocked her then. He had promised himself that day that he would never tell Shobha "because he still loved her then." (22) He told her the secret, "our baby was a boy. . . . His skin was more red than brown. He had black hair on his head. He weighed almost five pounds. His fingers were curled shut, just like yours in the night." (22) Shobha, non-plussed, turned the lights off. She came back to the table and sat down, and after a moment Sukumar joined her. The story ends with the words: "they wept together, for the things they now knew." (22)

The story reflects the alienation and loneliness that the emigrants face in a foreign land. The marriage bond, which is still considered sacrosanct in India, is gradually slithering down under the pressure of new needs under a different background. Nevertheless, one needs another's touch in an emotional crisis. That is why Shobha and Sukumar, failing to find any foothold of security, weep.

"When Mr. Pirzada Came to Dine" is the story of Mr. Pirzada, a professor from Bangladesh, doing research in America. He was a regular visitor to an Indian family in Boston. He was worried about the safety of his family in Bangladesh during 1971 war. He had left his wife and seven daughters without anybody to look after them in case of an eventuality. They were left to defend themselves. Naturally Mr. Pirzada looked worried and restless. Every day Lilia, the young daughter of the family, heard her father and Mr. Pirzada talking, discussing progress of the world that they watched on the T.V. Lilia was too young to understand the tension of the grown-ups, especially of Mr. Pirzada. Even she noticed her mother joining them. Lilia was left alone to observe: "most of all I remember the three of them operating during that time as if they were a single person, sharing a single man, a single body, a single silence and a single fear." (41) The story ends with Mr. Pirzada's returning to Bangladesh (Dacca), living in a free country with his wife and seven daughters. But Lilia missed him a lot; "Though I had not seen him for months, it was only then that I felt Mr. Pirzada's absence. It was only then, raising my water glass in his name, that I knew what it meant to miss someone who was so many miles and hours away, just as he had missed his wife." (42)

The title of the story has got romantic undertones although there is nothing romantic in the story. But it is difficult to understand the mind of Lilia who had very little connection with Mr. Pirzada, and Lilia was like one of his daughters left in Bangladesh. One is reminded of Ratan and Mini in Tagore's "The Postmaster" and "The Kabuliwalla." Lilia, although born and brought up in Boston, is unable to get rid of the sentiments, which Forster would call, absolutely Indian.

The title story "Interpreter of Maladies" is the story of an emigrant Indian family coming to India, especially to Orissa as tourists. Mr. and Mrs. Das with their three children, Tina, Mina and Bobby, come to Orissa and visit Puri, Konark and Khandagiri Udayagiri. Every year they visit their parents who are now living in Asansol. But the interpreter is the tourist guide cum car driver Mr. Kapasi and the story is more concerned about him than the tourists. Mr. Kapasi is an educated man who knows a little bit of French and other foreign languages. From his very young days, he used to act as an interpreter to the foreign tourists and this time he was with an emigrant Indian family from Boston. Mrs. Das came closer to Mr. Kapasi and she appreciated his work as an interpreter which his own wife looked down upon. This brought Mr. Kapasi closer to Mrs. Das and he compared her with his wife. At Konark, they moved together and engaged themselves in seeing erotic sculptures while Mr. Das was busy with the children in taking snaps. At Khandagiri, Mr. Das and the children went to the top of the mountain but Mrs. Das remained in the car. She felt tired. She came to the front seat and sat beside Mr. Kapasi. She told him the secret that Bobby was not Raj's son. She told him her relationship with her husband before and after marriage which very often left her lonely. The third child, Bobby, was not from an English man or an American but from an Indian, a Punjabi friend of Raj who came to stay with them for a week. She told him all this because she wanted an answer, a remedy for her. She said, "I was hoping you would help me feel better, say right thing. Suggest some kind of remedy." (65) Mr. Kapasi did not have any remedy with him for her. The only remedy that came to his mind was that she should be honest and tell the secret to Mr. Das. That also he did not suggest. He only asked her, "Is it really pain you feel, Mrs. Das or is it guilt?" (66) She only looked at him but did not say any thing. She opened the car door and went to meet her family. She wanted a readymade answer, a cure for her malady. But the malady is deep rooted and Mr. Kapasi, the interpreter, is no doctor to cure her of the malady. Most of the emigrant Indians suffer from different types of maladies and as Indians they are unable to get rid of their Indian consciousness that they should be honest and true to their married life. The concept of chastity (without understanding) haunts them like a ghost at noon. At the same time they cannot be completely westernized in their thoughts and feelings. This dichotomy is the predicament of the Indians settled abroad.

"A Real Darwan" is the story of Boori Ma, a watch woman, who is ultimately thrown out of the flat because of a theft. The people forget her honesty, her truthfulness. Her only fault was her garrulousness and she always boasted of her rich past and rich parents. The story is set in Bengal and it reminds us of a poem by Tagore "Puratan Bhrutuyu" (The old servant) although Boori Ma was not an idiot.

"Sexy" is the story based on an extra-marital relationship that Laxmi finds nauseating and absurd; Miranda gets herself involved with Dev in London. Emigrant Indians living abroad raise their eyebrows at this but cannot escape from it. The story reaches its climax when the son of Laxmi's cousin, who remains for some time with Miranda, asks her to wear the silver cock-tail dress that Miranda had once put on while going with Dev to a restaurant. She had to put on the dress as Rohin was adamant. When she came out in that dress he told her: "you are sexy." (107) She was taken aback. Dev had used the same word. She asked Rohin what he meant by the word sexy. Rohin reluctantly answered, "It means loving someone you don't know." (107) Rohin further said, "That's what my father did. . . . He sat next to someone he didn't know, someone sexy, and now he loves her instead of my mother." (108) This experience with the boy brought an end to her affair with Dev who was married. Perhaps Miranda came to realise that despite her smartness and beauty, she would not be the real cup of tea for Dev. Love does not mean to be sexy. It rather means being in each other's thoughts. Indians living abroad try to be smarter than the natives although they forget that in basic emotion there is hardly any difference between the East and the West. Even Lawrence never encouraged extramarital relationship in his novels. Sometimes emigrants, especially Indians, behave like upstarts. Although Jhumpa Lahiri is rarely explicit in her opinions or comments, nevertheless, there is always an undertone of irony in her stories.

"Mrs. Sen" is the story of another emigrant in America whose husband is a professor of mathematics in a university. The family is keenly observed by an American boy of eleven years named Eliot who is looked after by Mrs. Sen while his mother goes to work. Mrs. Sen's job is the job of a baby-sitter who has nothing to do at home except buying fish and cooking. Although the boy likes Mrs. Sen, he knows his mother is very critical of Mrs. Sen. She wants Mrs. Sen to go to her house but Mrs Sen does not know driving. She is learning driving. Eliot observes Mrs. Sen working at home. He is surprised to see the long, big, blade with which Mrs. Sen cuts vegetables and fish and she does not use knife which his mother always uses. She tells Eliot about the Indian marriage where women from neighbouring houses gather to cut vegetables the whole night amidst noise and merry-making. The American child is gradually exposed to the life of an Indian woman in her kitchen. Eliot feels the warmth in her voice and in her gait that he finds lacking in his mother. What he finds in Mrs. Sen, he does not find in his mother. Every evening after six, he is carried away by his mother in the car. He is appalled by the coldness of his mother to the warm hospitality of Mrs. Sen. The story comes to a climax when Mrs. Sen dashes her car against a telephone pole. Eliot is with her although no one is badly hurt. When Eliot's mother hears this, she stops Eliot from coming to Mrs. Sen any more. But the poignant part of the story is the intimacy that develops between Mrs. Sen and Eliot. Mrs. Sen has no friends in America. Her husband has no time for her. She tells Eliot how she feels lonely, how her golden dreams of living in a foreign land with her husband vanish like rain in summer. Eliot's mother, an American lady has no time at her disposal to realise the delicate emotion that develops between an American child and an Indian woman who takes time to adapt herself to a foreign country.

"The Blessed House" is the story of Sanjeeb and Twinkle; their new house at Connecticut where Sanjeeb worked; Twinkle completing her master's thesis at Stanford, a study of an Irish poet whom Sanjeeb had never heard of. Sanjeeb selected Twinkle and did not agree to marry anybody selected by her parents in Calcutta. Both were emigrants, although Sanjeeb had his parents in India and Twinkle in California. Twinkle's Indian connection was her name that sounded unusual to the ears of Douglas and Nora who came to the new house on the house-warming day. The new house was a blessed one as Twinkle found a statue of Christ and Mother Mary. The switch plates in the bed rooms were decorated with scenes from the Bible. Twinkle as a student of literature wanted to treasure those whereas Sanjeeb hated and disapproved of Twinkle's idea. This made him, almost, hate Twinkle as Sanjeeb, an executive in a firm, has no time to be bothered by such sentiments. To Twinkle, the house was a blessed house, to Sanjeeb, it was a cursed one. Sanjeeb felt that the interest for antic monuments in his wife was a temporary matter, just a device to come to the limelight as an Indian woman among the Americans. So the poor husband had nothing to do but "preserve the massive silver face to his ribs, careful not to let the feather hat slip, and followed her." (157)

"The Treatment of Bibi Haldar" is a poignant story that tells us the plight of Bibi Haldar who suffered from a baffling disease which made her family members exasperated, and ultimately she was left alone to suffer. The story is of Bengal. Bibi Haldar was staying with her relation in a flat in Calcutta. She was given a storage room on the roof, "a space in which one could sit but not comfortably stand, featuring an adjoining latrine, curtained entrance, one window without a grille, and shelves made from the panels of the old doors." (159) She recorded inventory for the cosmetics shop that her cousin Haldar owned and managed at the mouth of the courtyard. For her work she was given food, shelter and "sufficient metres of cotton at every October holiday to replenish her wardrobe and act as an inexpensive tailor." (159) Her only obsession in life was to get a husband. Every day she expected a man to come and offer his hand to her. It never materialized. She loved to hear from other women the details of their marriage. She would sigh after seeing their marriage albums. After devouring the details from other women, she would say, "when it happens to me, you will all be present." (160) After futile waiting, she would say, "My face will never be painted with sandalwood paste, who will rub me with turmeric? My name will never be printed with scarlet ink on a card." (160-61) But Mr. and Mrs. Haldar never cared to give any thought to this although Mr. Haldar gave an advertisement after being pestered by the inmates of the flat. Mrs. Haldar, who was in family way, feared Bibi as an evil omen and wanted to get rid of her shadow lest it brought harm to her child. She gave birth to a female child. She froze with fear when her daughter suffered for five days. At last Mr. Haldar winded up his cosmetic shop and left the place with his wife and the daughter. Bibi was left alone with Rs. 300 that Mr. Haldar left with her. But the story takes a turn when the inmates find, after Mr. and Mrs. Haldar's departure, that Bibi Haldar was pregnant. The search for the real culprit ended in futility. She delivered a male child and took care of the child. The story ends with these words, "she was, to the best of her knowledge, cured." (172)

"The Third and Final Continent" is the last story in the collection that moves from London to Boston and gives to the readers a different taste. Although the same emigrant themes—the initial hurdles to settle, to adjust and after sometimes trying to be more native than the natives—the story tells us the strange encounter of a Bengali commerce graduate who moves from Calcutta to London and then to Boston with an old woman of 100 years, Mrs. Croft, in whose house he lodges as a tenant. The old American lady was proud of her own country when America landed on the moon. To her the achievement was "splendid" and she wanted the Bengali gentleman to say the word clearly. She was alone and her daughter Helen made weekend visit to her with provisions for the week. The old lady was very particular about the rent which was to be paid on Friday. She let out her rooms only to bachelors from Harvard or Tech. She belonged to old America who reacted to the long chats by his daughter and the narrator. She did not approve of a woman talking to a bachelor for a long time. It must have sounded unbelievable to Indian ears who come to America with all ideas of an advanced society where, they think, permissiveness is the rule. But Mrs. Croft belongs to the values of old America. The narrator left her home and moved to a new apartment when Mala, his wife, came to him from India. The old lady is dead; the narrator's son goes to college and the child born in America of Indian origin looks askance at the sentimentality of his father. He is born in America to establish an identity of his own; to live as a naturalised citizen of America—an emigrant, although the umbilical chord is still rooted in India and it is difficult to sever it altogether. The story ends with the rumination of the father: "whenever he is discouraged, I tell him that if I can survive on three continents, then there is no obstacle he cannot conquer. While the astronauts, heroes forever, spent mere hours on the moon, I have remained in this new world for nearly thirty years. I know that my achievement is quite ordinary. I am not the only man to seek his fortune far from home, and certainly I am not the last. Still, there are times I am bewildered by each mile I have traveled, each meal I have eaten, each person I have known, each room in which I have slept. As ordinary as it all appears, there are times when it is beyond my imagination." (197-98)

This is the fear and anxiety that remains with an emigrant despite his best efforts to beat the natives in dress, gestures and postures. All the time, there is a feeling of being alienated. It is primarily because he can neither cut off the sweet silken bond that ties him to the land of his origin or his parents. Jhumpa Lahiri is undoubtedly the first emigrant writer who is concerned with their maladies and tries to be an interpreter. Of course, she is quite different from Mr. Kapasi. She probes deep into the maladies but prescribes no cure. She is an artist and the artist's another name is an interpreter. The stories reveal the skill Jhumpa Lahiri has achieved in her maiden venture. There is no chronological or sequential development of stories. She has evolved her own style by changing the mode of narration from past to the present and again reversing it without being nostalgic. Her style is almost cinematic and with the help of montage one gets a glimpse into the meaning of the story One reading is not enough to understand any of her stories.

Crisis in Human Values as Reflected in Jhumpa Lahiri's *Interpreter of Maladies*

JYOTI MISHRA

Since the beginning of the civilization, every society had lived by certain human values and beliefs. These human values had gone into making the society more firm and solid. In olden times, people generally abided by these values at any cost. They had the fear of god. They believed in heaven and hell. But with the advent of science and technology, human mentality changed. The existence of Almighty was put to question and people now stopped looking to a life beyond the present one. So there developed a common tendency that, whatever is to be achieved, it is to be achieved only in this very life. 'Dharma' and 'Moksha' became futile and on the other hand 'Kama' and 'Artha' acquired prominence in human life. Subsequently, the human values changed and there arose crisis.

Under such state of affairs, what could the Indian writing in English today reflect other than the irony and the suffering of the common man caught in social contradiction. It made the writers sad but then they were exploring the present time in the perspective of Indian tradition and history.

Jhumpa Lahiri is one such writer, a dazzling story teller with a distinctive voice, an eye for nuance and an ear for irony. She has very sublimely understated in her collection of short stories entitled, *Interpreter of Maladies*, the lives of Indians in exile, of people navigating between the strict tradition they have inherited and the baffling new world they must encounter every day. *Interpreter of Maladies* is her first published collection which bagged her the Pulitzer Prize for Fiction 2000. From the above collection the two stories under consideration for this paper are: "A Temporary Matter" and "Interpreter of Maladies."

"A Temporary Matter" is the story of Shobha and Sukumar, a young couple, who had lived in Boston for three years. Shobha worked in an office downtown where she searched for typographical errors. Sukumar was in the sixth year of his graduate school and was to enter the job market the following year. For some time, their life was not so happy as they had lost their baby who was born dead. Moreover, as Sukumar thought,

> how he and Shobha had been experts at avoiding each other in their three-bedroom house, spending as much time on separate floors as possible. He thought of how he no longer looked forward to weekends . . . and how long it had been since she looked into his eyes and smiled or whispered his names on those rare occasions they still reached for each other before sleeping.

So the more Shobha stayed out putting in extra hours at work, the more Sukumar wanted to stay in managing the household matters.

Under such state of affairs, crisis in their married life continued when a 'temporary matter' in the form of a notice broke in. It informed them about the five-days's power cut off for one hour. This unexpected announcement provided them a chance to come closer to each other once again. Unable to think anything in particular about spending an hour in darkness, Shobha turned nostalgic and said, "I remember during power failures at my grandmother's house, we all had to say something. A little poem. A joke. A fact about the world." So, she suggested, "let us, say something to each other in the dark. How about telling each other, something we've never told before."

Having thus decided, Sukumar and Shobha started revealing their untold facts to each other. Shobha told him about the times when they were newly acquainted and when she happened to steal a look into his address book to see if he had written her address there. Sukumar in his turn told her about how he had forgotten to tip the waiter when they went out to dinner for the first time and how the next morning he went all the way back just to tip the waiter.

Somehow the whole affair had turned into an exchange of confessions—the little ways they had hurt or disappointed each other. The following nights Sukumar told her about how he once ripped out a photo of a woman in one of the fashion magazines and carried it in his books for a week. He revealed to her how he hadn't lost the sweater vest Shobha bought him for their third wedding anniversary but had exchanged it for cash at Filene's and that he had got drunk in the middle of the day at a hotel bar.

Confession of each other's guilts was not all that the couple did but they also engaged themselves in some amount of love-making they had forgotten. Eventually, Sukumar started looking forward to the lights going out so much so that he was really disappointed when he came to know that the fault was repaired one day ahead of schedule.

The process of confession which started in the dark continued even in the light, for they had now developed the courage to face each other, and they no more required the veil of darkness. As a result, a startling revelation came from the side of Shobha when she said that she had signed a lease for a separate accommodation which she had been looking for some time before. Sukumar was sickened to realize that the game of confession was purposely designed by Shobha only to make her matters easy. He then took his turn and disclosed something he had sworn he would never tell his wife. It was about the sex of their child that Shobha herself had wanted to be a surprise until it was born. The final confession from either side was thus made. Shobha who had initiated all this burst into tears and Sukumar also joined her.

The crisis in the life of Shobha and Sukumar that simmered in the form of lack of love as faith in their interpersonal-relationship and Shobha's efforts for isolated living came out through confession. But then these confessions proved a bliss in disguise—a bliss that cleared their hearts and brought them together once again

"Interpreter of Maladies" is the title story where Mr. Kapasi, a driver-cum-Interpreter guided an American family of Mr. Das, accompanied by his wife and three children to the Sun Temple, Konark. On his way to the temple, Mr. Kapasi told them about his other job, the job of an interpreter in a doctor's clinic. He said that he interpreted peoples's maladies, translated the symptoms of the Gujarati patients to the non-Gujarati doctor. Mr. Das had never heard of anything like that and Mrs. Das in particular remarked that it was a romantic one, a big responsibility, as the patients were totally dependent on him. Mr. Kapasi had never thought of his job in such complimentary terms. To him it was a sign of his failings as he had dreamed of being an interpreter for diplomats and dignitaries, resolving conflicts between people and nations.

Apart from everything else, Mr. Kapasi was a keen observer. He saw that Mrs. Das did not behave in a romantic way towards her husband and was not much concerned about her children as well. He wondered if Mr. and Mrs. Das were a bad match. Flattered by her praises, Mr. Kapasi started taking interest in Mrs. Das. He was anxious to be alone with her and indulge in some private conversation. He began to dread the thought of dropping the family off to the hotel from were he had picked them. So, on their way back, he suggested visiting the hills at Udayagiri and Khandagiri to which they agreed. When they got to the hills, Mrs. Das refused to get out of the car, whereas Mr. Das left the place along with the children. When left alone in the car with Mr. Kapasi, Mrs. Das made an astonishing revelation that one of her boys named Bobby was not her husband's son but his friend's son. She said that she had kept it a secret for eight years and had not even let her husband know about it. But concealing it from everyone was not easy for her as she constantly felt terrible. She developed an unhealthy state of mind and had a strange urge of throwing things away.

Moving in such a state of mind, Mrs. Das found Mr. Kapasi's role of interpreter promising enough to lighten the burden of her heart. She hoped that he would help her feel better by saying the right thing or suggesting some kind of remedy. Mr.

Kapasi, on his part, could make out that it was not her pain pouring out but it was her confession of guilt. Not used to such kind of maladies, the interpreter "still believed that it was his duty to assist Mrs. Das. Perhaps he ought to tell her to confess the truth to Mr. Das. He would explain that honesty was the best policy, which would surely help her feel better." His thoughts remained locked in his mind, as he didn't find a chance to convey his remedy to Mrs. Das. But the solution to the crisis was successfully conveyed through the 'interpreter of maladies' to the readers.

Jhumpa Lahiri's *Interpreter of Maladies*: Interpreting Human Values

MADHOO KAMARA

Tasmāc Chastrain Pramānam
Kāry ākryā—Vyavasthitau
Thātvā Sāstra—Vidhān Oktain
Karma Kartum inharhasi (*Bhagvad Gita*, XV: 24)

(Let the scriptures be your norm in determining what should be done and what not. Understand the injunction of the scriptures first and then set yourself to work.)

Is modern Indian English novel a variegated phenomenon which tries to catch reflection of what Sri Aurobindo has called, "the orange skies of the Mystic Mind"? Is it true that the modern Indian English novelists through fear and frenzy have bungled and brought this darkness called the "Shunya" upon us? Should we—the recipients—diet on negation of traditional socio-cultural values and live still in the dark before the right movement and affirmation may be possible. The horror-terror-pity evocating thought that there is "crisis in human values in Indian writing in English is to me mathematically unplausible." We should remember the time-tested pronouncement—"An author is literature: not scripture."

Certainly the spirit of India is dominated by ruthless technology; the simple human nature is tossed between the fire of greed and the ice of 'hate' but the tremendous equation "tatwamasi" does establish a correspondence between the world "within" and the world "outside." Our modern Indian English writers came very near the Aurobindonian ideal of a theme creator of art:

> the true poet shows us truth in its Power of beauty in its symbol of image or reveals it to us in the workings of life, and when he has done that his whole work is done he need not be an explicit spokesman.

William Meredith's tribute to Frost's poetic craftsmanship fitly describes the new form of the Indian English writing: "It has grown like a tree of new species, the layer of live wood is a perennial miracle of new life, but the tree itself is what is altogether astonishing—'a new tree.'"

Certainly, it strives to affirm in fierce imaginative terms that man will yet redeem himself and his fellows in spite of the present perversions and egoisms and that the world will endure the present social ills.

Transition is not decay. The 'Sat' the permanently existent values like the truthfulness, tranquillity, aversion to slander, freedom from sensuality, gentleness, modesty, steadfastness, vigour, patience and fortitude are 'centrifugal' although the 'Asat'—the unreal fleeting environs—has become centripetal. The Asat has become trendy and relates to "Existentialism," "The Absurd," "The Surrealism" and the like. Here lies the clue, no matter what the resources are, the sadhana of the Great Taskmaster's eye continues to uphold; "Thou was not born for death, O immortal bird!"

The present study is a product of my exploration of *Interpreter of Maladies* by Jhumpa Lahiri, one of the few flagbearers of Indian English fiction whose genius as a story-teller has been appreciated by all. She has brought a strikingly fresh sensibility to Indian English literature, broadening impressively the thematic and stylistic contours of art. The present paper explores her as a new consciousness articulating and emphasizing the impermanence of values, inherent emotions, and philosophical echoes. Therefore, her contribution to the genre of Indian short story is truly impressive.

Interpreter of Maladies is a collection of nine stories of which "A Temporary Matter" is the opening one. It records the process of restoration of faith after a long dividing doldrum—a threat to the otherwise gloomy conjugality of unwanted interdependency between Sukumar and Shobha. Sukumar with his elusive nature and Shobha with her professional specificity create discord that prevails for a moderate length of time and finally devours all unhappiness, leaving fertile bond to revive the long lost hope and reassemble conjugal bliss. Consequently, all mental doubts and apprehensions that cloud their life's guideposts are unweeded and the aesthetics of good compensates for the temporary loss of happiness.

"When Mr. Pirzada Came to Dine" epitomizes universal oneness—Vishwabandhutva—the elixir of peaceful and perfect living. Here, moralistic orientation forms the basis of constructive living, along with secular rationality and social solidarity. These human values infuse 'Positivism' in a wretched father of seven daughters left all to their fate along with their mother, in Dacca—a country "invaded, torched and shelled by the Pakistani army." The elements of Paramartha surface on every page vibrating the reader with the throbs of a heart in destitute, but earnest in the process of well-wishing. Reunion of Mr. Pirzada with his family proclaims the novelist's belief in collective mental and moral energies—the core meaning of "Loka Samskar Sukhino Bhavantu."

"A Real Durvan" is a beautiful synthesis of thought and character. A note of despair prevails all through the length of the story to be resolved at the end by a marked optimism. The protagonist named Boori Ma is an emaciated old woman who voluntarily serves as a watchman in a multi-storeyed building in Calcutta. Her present is rooted in dead past as memoirs of lost royalty and grandeur. Jhumpa Lahiri projects a meaningful integrity functional in bettering existence as vital and potent in combating survival odds. The "Chaos" is henceforth saved by virtue of 'Cosmos' and the ideal integrity envelops the purposive individual supported by harmonic 'dharma' in the living forms of

Mrs. and Mr. Dalal. Jointly they stand against the destructive practical selfishness of the inmates of the big building.

Transformation of the 'force within' through the purgatorial trials and tribulations is the theme of the story "Sexy." Miranda realizes the mean, the animal and the irrational within her and soon mends her way to rise up to the heights of nobility which again is a moral medal. The story also emphasizes that awareness of righteousness is an achievement of a conscientious soul. This is the necessary deep-structure theme.

"The Blessed Home" voices the idea that man's ever-ending task is to discover his limitations and to atone for the deficiencies of human life and surroundings. The story also elaborates the idea that success lies in our willingness to construct an adaptive and assimilative living, further to reconstruct "what has fallen apart"; if any. Here Twinkle and Sanjeev violate their convictions but are soon convinced that the joy of togetherness can only be consistent when proper room is shaped to accommodate mutual desires and demands. The advantage and necessity of interpersonal dependence is also focussed to express necessary participation in marital life, otherwise estrangement is the unavoidable catastrophe.

"Bibi Haldar" clinically examines the world of meaningless interpersonal relations "within a family" but meaningful affirmation "within a society" that aids the sublimations of a wretched soul of 'a convulsing girl' to the state of blessedness. The group sensitivity is contrasted to domestic emotional numbness destructive enough to dismantle the airy pleasure dome of Bibi Haldar. Her single solitary living, her mawkish soliloquies and her maudlin sentiments are an endless worry to the reciprocative neighbourhood. 'Vasudha ev Kutumbakam' is the rescuing force and the potential of the feeling of a neighbourhood is the foregrounded element.

The title story "Interpreter of Maladies" is an in-depth study of socio-human relationship. The story registers the common-day-today bickering between a couple on the issue of attending upon yet-to-grow kids. Mr. and Mrs. Das along with their children—Tina, Ronny and Bobby—are on their visit to the Sun Temple at

Konark. Mr. Kapasi, their escort to the Sun Temple, finds them quaint in their dress and interpersonal relationship. Against the shade of excellent imagery, the story reads hurriedly as the curiosity mounts with the advancement of narration by the omniscient narrator. The long tedious journey is made pleasant by the experiences of the Interpreter and by his recollections of his past marital life against his observation of the cordiality between Mr. and Mrs. Das. Here Lahiri pinpoints the large-heartedness of Indians in encompassing even foreigners within their socio-cultural realm of interaction.

Further, under the effect of 'universal love' and 'universal energy,' Mrs. Das confides in Mr. Kapasi that Bobby is not Mr. Das's son but of his friend to whom she surrendered in a swirl of passion when her husband was out on his daily work. The loom of 'pativratadharma' nags her and she longs for "atmasamarpna"—of merging one's personality in another's—an account of "Aatmaglani." She says: "About my secret, and about how terrible it makes me feel. I feel terrible looking at my children and at Raj, always terrible." She adds, "It means that I'm tired of feeling so terrible all the time. Eight years, Mr. Kapasi, I've been in pain." This is how, trapped in the sterility of custom and tradition, the individuals struggle for their comprehension of the destiny, some discovery of interpersonal ties, some metaphor of meaningful selfhood and withering charm of one's being in a socio-cultural context. Her primary interest lies in the nature and quality of the human consciousness alongwith substantial emphasis on stories, on the steady flow of outward landscape and on the changing reality. We are made aware of the process of change, how it affects 'living,' viewed both from an internal and external focus:

> Shobha looked at him now, her face contorted with sorrow. He had cheated on a college exam, ripped a picture of women out of a magazine. He had returned a sweater and got drunk in the middle of the day instead. These were the things he had told her. He had held her son who had known life only within her against his chest in a darkened

> room in an unknown wing of the hospital . . . he still loved her then and it was the one thing in her life that she wanted to be a surprise. (22)

For this, Lahiri abstracts the temporal canvas of the Indian as well as emigrant life into an elaborate picture made luminous in the consciousness of a single person who either happens to be the narrator as in "When Mr. Pirzada Came to Dine" or the lives narrated as in "Sexy," "Mrs. Sen's," "A Temporary Matter," etc. endowed with special gifts of lyric insight, image and encompassing sympathy. Through this narrative emphasis on the individual's inner psyche, we are launched into the existentialistic wilderness where we find the images and glimpses of our true nature. Her stories do not reflect upon the cumulative sequences of life. Rather, they offer indiscreet moments of truth as they affect individual lives and build up a fairly consistent view of man and his world. Using short stories as epiphanies, Jhumpa reveals the social and culture turmoil with the being as theme in focus.

Interpreter of Maladies also reveals Jhumpa Lahiri's capacity to transmute commonplace objects and ordinary experiences derived from the natural and human worlds into symbols of deeper speculative meaning. For example, the image of Boori Ma in "A Real Durvan" stands for eternal endurance and patience of India, baffling unending threats to its metaphysical richness. With her gentleness, compassion and exuberant love, she is a matriarchal figure, an apotheosis of Indian history and culture. Similarly, Mrs. Croft in "The Third Final Continent" stands for the superior and the mysterious; the noble exalted to the love of the sacred.

Jhumpa Lahiri's stories are the impressive explorations of the human conditions as it shapes and is shaped by the varying textuality of the human personality and offer testimony to her interest in creating an organic evolvement of both 'the content' and the 'form.' For example, "Sexy" voices existential despair. More painful than the physical hardships is the emotional trauma of separation. Her tragic lot lies in her willingness to fail as a beloved of a married man. The story is a powerful rebuttal to the commonly held notion that youthful girls are nasty "familial home wreckers."

The backdrop adds to the charm. India, America, Boston and Dacca are the changing landscapes but the tumultuous happening within the human and social worlds creates a universal story of love and unhappiness. The book also contains the drama with many of our key traits—self-assertion, self-negation, self-awareness, family ties, vanity and hatred which makes us feel that an imperfect human brain breeds dissonance in living pattern. The principle of causation and illustration highlights the necessity of introspection and improvement. The greatness of the book lies in the style, structure and accuracy in making the tale of human idiosyncrasies thought-provoking and soul-searching. Jhumpa Lahiri does not explicitly point out the remedy. She has presented people as they are, but it teaches the lesson of humility, equality and motivates us to retain the good of past in the face of the challenges of life with the head held high. Almost all stories end on a positive note, with the hope of a 'tomorrow' which suggests that with little efforts we can discard our shallow pretensions and move towards a society where the traditional and the modern world meet in their inherent goodness, asserting the worth of a human life.

The rise of a new sensibility accompanied by the growth of a peripheral mind is interpreted as "loss of moral perception," eroding thoughts of nobility. On the contrary, "the growth of the ideal" now exemplifies the Indian mind transferred by knowledge, not of good and evil, but of a world that has for the first time photographed, measured, explored, analyzed and counted to relate a consciousness incredibly widened and deepened and justified for man's view of the world. In the evolution of this consciousness after Tagore and Aurobindo, R.K. Narayan, M.R. Anand, Kamala Markandaya, Anita Desai, Bharati Mukherjee, Arundhati Roy and Jhumpa Lahiri are the friends and the makers, certainly "The Paradise" is not lost. In the labyrinths of past rather it has evolved as "cosmic weather," a reflection of some glorious to which the modern writers are discoverers.

The body of literature to which these writers have devoted to give permanent form remain history of our age and provide means, for the next age, to transcend the nightmarish crisis in human values to the idyllic past in the present. Hence modern Indian English literature is profoundly moral. Its real aim is to redeem reality through art without being preachy or pious. It is a way through 'Shunya' to 'Ghayna.' Ihab Hassan writes: "In great literature, there is no past, and no built-in obsolescence. There is radical continuity. We cannot afford to live in the perishable present without knowledge, deep passionate knowledge of the continuous present. Men like Yeats, Lawrence, Kafka and Faulkner are still prophets of the continuous present. They tell us who we are and how we could live." (*The American Review*, October 1967, New Delhi)

The Nowhere Women: The Quest for Identity in Manorama Mathai's *Mulligatawny Soup*

URBASHI BARAT

Manorma Mathai's *Mulligatawny Soup*[1] purports to be a disquisition in fictional guise on the plight of the Anglo-Indians, that minuscule community of half-castes uneasily straddling the two worlds to which it is tied by bonds as indissoluble as they are invisible, yet uncomfortably aware that it belongs to neither; a community that is as much the marker of the clash and the merger of two disparate cultures as the mulligatawny soup of the title. In a world in which assertion of ethnic identity is a politically correct move and multiculturalism/multiracialism the favourite buzzword, Mathai's novel makes all the right noises. Never mind, of course, that it is a rehash of a popular two-decade-old Hindi film "Julie"; never mind, too, that it reinforces all the old stereotypes about Anglo-Indians (the railway colony, the hard-drinking father, the aggressive mother, the promiscuity in the mating games of the young, the ubiquitous references to Home); never mind if its attempt to reproduce the characteristic Anglo-Indian dialect and speech rhythms is frequently forced and unnatural (for instance, 'mater' and 'pater' rather than the more commonly used 'Mummy' and 'Daddy,' the injection of 'man' into the dialogue whenever Mathai can manage it, and, rather irritatingly, the indiscriminate use of the Anglo-Indian plural form of 'you,' 'you all,' for both singular and plural). The fashionable nostalgia for the Raj and sympathy for a vanishing tribe couples with a suitably exotic set of characters to provide Mathai's novel enough interest for the reviewers to dissect it.

The fact remains, however, that as a novel about the Anglo-Indians, *Mulligatawny Soup* is hardly more than a bundle of clichés, barely rising above the level of journalese; the artistic success of Allan Sealy's *Trotter Nama* casts a long shadow over it, and makes its study of the world of the Anglo-Indians an outsider's view, simplistic and superficial by comparison. The narrator's occasional lapses in style, the recourse to Indianisms quite inappropriate for a girl born and bred in England in an English family, with no intimacy with Indians, moreover, takes away from the novelist's attempt at verisimilitude, just as the long insertions about the history of the characteristics of the Anglio-Indians tend to turn the novel into a kind of tract. The author, furthermore, seems to have little knowledge about the India she writes about: Shahpur belongs to Forster's India rather than to India's north-east, Sen is not a Brahmin surname among the Bengalis, nor is Tarla a Bengali name; Nikhil Sen's encounter with the railway guard Horatio Ronby is straight out of Gandhiji's life, while Tarla Sen's speeches to her dolls are a replica of Indira Gandhi's childhood days.

Yet it would be hasty to write off *Mulligatawny Soup* as a failure. Once the novel is read not as the story of the Anglo-Indian community but as a female bildungsroman that presents the woman's quest for identity, once, in D.H. Lawrence's phrase, we trust, not the teller, but the tale, the Anglo-Indian background becomes a metaphor for the dangling woman, yearning for selfhood, and making a place for herself by learning to rise above heartbreak and failure. This is the theme of the bildungsroman form as it is of the woman's novel. Juliet Mitchell explains: "Roughly speaking, the novel starts with autobiographies written by women in the seventeenth century. . . . These writers were trying to establish what critics today call the 'subject in process.' What they were trying to do was to create a history from a state of flux, a flux in which they were feeling themselves in the process of becoming women within a new bourgeois society. . . . The novel is that creation by the woman of the woman."[2]

Like many bildungsromans, and like the female bildungsroman in particular, *Mulligatawny Soup* is narrated in the first person. But, interestingly enough, the narrator is not the protagonist; she is someone who meets the protagonist in the course of her own quest for selfhood and who recognizes the protagonist's story as being in many ways an ironic counterpart to her own. She may disclaim her own involvement in the protagonist's life, but as she retells Elsie-Nora Ronby's tale in the hope that it will help to "make sense of it all, for myself," (3) she realizes that "we were not as dissimilar as I had first thought, and I took the decision to write about her, sort of juxtaposed with me. We were both in-betweens with a strong sense that we did not belong." (6) What we have here, then, is a double-bildungsroman plot which, through its intricate meshing of different lives, different worlds, suggests that what is explored in the novel is woman's place, woman's life, and not merely the life-story of a single individual or a single community.

The narrator begins Elsie-Nora's story by prefacing it with her own. She is the child of an English mother and an Indian father, who had deserted his wife in England before she was born—an ironic re-enactment of the way in which English soldiers in the early days of the Raj had so often tricked and abandoned their Indian families, whose descendants were to form the Anglo-Indian community later. It also parallels the way in which Elsie-Nora herself is jilted twice over. The two men in her life belong to the two different communities whose temporary union produced her own; no matter, then, to which social or ethnic group she belongs, or the age in which she lives, woman exists to be exploited, used and cast away—until, like Elsie-Nora, she learns to grow beyond acceptance and rejection and make her own life on her own terms.

Growing up coloured in multiracial Camden Town has not been too hard for the narrator. What has been difficult to accept, rather, is the rejection she has faced by the immediate members of her family, whose "joint witness" (3) excludes her in a way the outside world does not (in contemporary Britain after all, pluralism is fashionable)—symptomatic of a society in which conformity is more important than selfhood, especially for women. Neither can she identify with the Indian women on the

London streets who may not know India at all (like the Ugandan refugees) but who cling so tenaciously to their Indianness, even though this makes them permanent aliens in their chosen homes. Consequently she begins to question "who [she] was and where [she] actually belonged." (2) hoping to discover her "Indian father's India" (3) and "exorcise' his ghost from her life." (1)

At first when she meets her protagonist, Elsie-Nora's background seems to be very different from her own postcolonial middle-class London suburb, in which racialism is rarely overt. Elsie-Nora, however, was born and brought up in the small town of Shahpur during the last decades of the Raj, a town which, unlike Camden Town, observed strict social segregation. Where the narrator has never known her natural father and feels alienated from her stepfather, Elsie-Nora is the third daughter of a railway guard and a hospital nurse, both fiercely proud of the 'Anglo' part of their ancestry, and dreaming of going Home one day to an England that had never been and would never be a real home to them.

Indeed, the highest ambition that Mrs. Ronby could aspire to for her daughters was that they would marry Englishmen and live in England in the grand style they had seen Englishmen adopting in India. Mrs. Ronby is thus Mathai's counterpart to Jane Austen's Mrs. Bennet; the similarity extends also to the way her two older daughters have married, one prudently, to an Englishman who has taken her Home with him, and the other foolishly, to an Anglio-Indian even lower down the social ladder than the Ronbys. Annis Pratt's comments are relevant here: "The supreme goal of these novels of development [the female bildungsromans] is to groom the young hero for marriage, and whereas younger girls are given tests in submission in a general way, their older sisters are provided with models of behavior appropriate for success in the marriage market."[3] Ginevra and Gloria are therefore models for Elsie-Nora, to learn what to do and what not to do.

The role of Constantia Ronby in the novel and in Elsie-Nora's life is paralleled by her English godmother Elinor Graham, who can adjust neither to the new India nor to the new

England and by that of Hugh Walker's mother in his. Juxtaposed against them are the faceless Indian mother in Tarla and Tarun Sen's family—their mother and their grandmother—who also use their own brand of emotional blackmail to get their own way. As Gilbert and Gubar point out, "the 'hunger strike' is a traditional tool of the powerless, as the history of the feminist movement (and many other movements of oppressed peoples) will attest."[4] Because the Western women believe they have some power over their lives and their families, they do not resort to the hunger strike, perhaps, but their way is equally the victim's way, the way of what Margaret Atwood described as the victim who denies her own victimization.[5]

In the certainties of the settled hierarchical world of Shahpur, Elsie-Nora's position is secure and assured until one day she is forced to recognize that in fact she belongs nowhere. This happens when the Anglo-Indian girls in school are busy at their old game of showing the Indian girls how lowly their position in the social ladder is, and suddenly one of their victims, Tarla Sen, the firebrand daughter of a wealthy freedom-fighter, points out that the Anglo-Indians are always the losers, for they are neither fish nor flesh. (18-19) This is the first time that she discovers the anomalies of her position, and she is even more shocked to discover that far from taking her side, the English girls are actually laughing at her. This incident starts her on her journey of self-discovery: the first betrayal is always the first step towards identity and selfhood for the bildungsroman protagonist.

A strange friendship begins to grow between the two erstwhile enemies, the Anglo-Indian and the Indian, but this is a relationship that soon collapses under the weight of contradictions and time. Where Tarla learns to attend public meetings and quote Sarojini Naidu, Elsie-Nora enters the fascinating but dangerous world of adult joys, of sexual games and titillation in the hunt for a husband. The one thing they continue to share, without realizing it, is that both are engaged in a search, a search for a meaning in life, a search for identity, one that each pursues in the only way open to her under the circumstances.

When they catch up with each other again, neither has found her place, though Elsie-Nora is working as a secretary in a British firm and Tarla planning to study in the England that she and her family had so unequivocally rejected before Independence. The Anglo-Indian girl points out the irony of "the need to find ourselves again, to ask ourselves who we are . . . to discover ourselves,"[5] which Tarla expresses, so far away from home; but the Indian can only reiterate her friend's lack of identity: "Now here's you, living like an outsider in what should be your own country and you despise the greater part of yourself because you have been taught that the only worthwhile part of you is your little Anglo bit." (51) She attempts to heal the breach by inviting Elsie-Nora to a party at her house, something that she had not dared to do before Independence and before adulthood—indeed, it had been her inability to invite an Anglo-Indian to her birthday party that had caused the childhood rift between them—and the latter accepts.

At the party she finds once again that she does not belong, by virtue of both her socio-economic class and her racial origin; but to ease her discomfort there is the masculine admiration for her looks that she perceives, while Tarla's brother Tarun, home from Cambridge for the long vacation, is obviously smitten by her. Tarla tries to warm her off by telling her that her mother has already chosen a bride for her easy-going and obedient son—"that's the Indian way" (58)—underlining the fact that it is clearly not the Anglo-Indian one. But she apparently also sees the need to "integrate" her friend (61) into India, and goes on to ask her to join her club of intellectuals.

Elsie-Nora is obviously no intellectual, but she agrees to the suggestion, partly out of curiosity, partly because she feels it might further her search for selfhood, for the club would widen her horizons. But she also continues to see Tarun, not just because she genuinely likes the unpretentious young man but also because he seems to be her passport to an affluent Indian life style and to belonging somewhere. (63-64) She wonders how to "bind him to a commitment. She knew so little of him outside their meetings that she was unable to visualize herself in his life, could conjure up no picture of herself in his home, with his parents, or even with his friends to whom she had never been introduced." (68) She even agrees to wear a sari to please him, though it angers her mother, who sees no future in a relationship which only threatens her Anglo-Indian identity.

The turning-point comes when she calls on Tarun unexpectedly and overhears the caustic comments of his father about herself (the mother, interestingly, is not so harsh). As she runs away from the house, Tarun goes after her and proposes to her in a rush, but his quick, furtive embrace is an indication of the nature of his feelings, and suggestive of the fate of their relationship. The matter, of course, comes to its expected conclusion with Tarun succumbing to parental pressure, marrying the girl chosen for him by the family and returning to England, leaving behind a letter for Elsie-Nora to be delivered by his sister. The betrayal by the brother and the sister spells the end of Elsie-Nora's attempts to find her own place in India through marriage to an Indian. Her parents may be pleased, but the girl herself is unhappy, humiliated and discouraged, and begins to feel that "there was no future for her in India, no prospect of bettering herself." (79) Marriage, then, is the only option for the women, the only career, the only means of fulfilment and of achieving autonomy and identity. This is as true for Elsie-Nora as it is for Sushma, who has to cope with a husband with a roving eye, or even for Tarla, whose search has ended by her obediently falling in love with the erudite and apparently very suitable but equally unattractive—physically as well as morally, as it turns out later—Dr. Jagdish Bannerji, whom she calls *dada*, 'elder brother,' and therefore someone with whom, from the Indian/Hindu point of view, who should not have been romantically involved at all. Outside marriage there is only the workplace, where sexual harassment is the norm, and not only if the victim is Anglo-Indian, as Elsie-Nora is to discover later.

England is the only hope, she feels, but Ginevra is unencouraging. Then one ray of light enters her purblind world, as Robert Grant, a young Englishman freshly arrived in India, becomes her boss. Robert does not understand the difference between her and the Indians around him, why she "seem[s] such an outsider, almost a foreigner like himself in India," (89) and he expects her to be a guide to the country: a role she has never assumed before and in which she is completely out of place. Nevertheless, and in spite of knowing that he has a girlfriend back in England, she tries to entice him: "she recognized that this would probably be her last chance, as her mother kept telling her, and it was up to her to do something about it." (87) They are soon on friendly terms, and, delighted, her parents insist she invite him home for dinner.

The dinner is comic for the reader, but it is a disaster for Elsie-Nora. Robert is alarmed and disgusted by her family and their house, and begins to withdraw. Matters take another turn at another party; it is interesting to note the role of the party in Elsie-Nora's progress, for parties and feasting are the traditional symbols of celebrating belonging. Both her previous boss, who had tried to seduce her earlier, and Tarla's husband are present. They lose no time in describing her as a "good-time girl" and a "gold-digger like all her tribe" (115)—and there is from one point of view sufficient truth in these accusations—and Robert prefers to believe them rather than what he himself has seen of her. After all, this makes things so much more convenient; now he can without a twinge of conscience turn their relationship into a physical one, in which he is the conqueror, the colonizer, reenacting what his country and his sex had done to India and to women through the centuries. Elsie-Nora becomes the acquiescient victim in Margaret Atwood's account, (37-38) and the narrator comments: "Many of us women have, or think they have, little but our bodies to offer and so it is only natural that we put a high price on this, our beauty, expecting to barter it for love, security, happiness, even a career. . . . In Elsie-Nora's case, it might also have been that she valued her body so little that she saw no harm in offering it in exchange for a possible passage to England. Elsie-Nora manages, however, to survive. With Robert Grant's departure, she resolves to start afresh, choosing to escape from her little provincial town to Delhi in characteristic bildungsroman fashion, in which, as Jerome H. Buckley points out in *Season of Youth*,[6] the protagonist's *bildung* begins with the move from the countryside of the provinces to the sophistication and ambiguities of a metropolis. In order to make the break with her past more complete, she even assumes a new identity and a new name, Sinara Ranbir; and she is surprised to discover what a difference just a change of nomenclature can make in people's attitudes. (124) She is accepted in a way she had never been before. It is uncomfortable to pretend that she is an Indian, but she is anxious to discover her Indian selfhood buried by generations of acknowledging only the English part. What she finds, however, is not Indianness but gender politics. Just because she is a single female, she remains 'fair game' for men. It is not her Anglo-Indian background, then, but her gender itself that is the cause of her victimization. This realization marks another important step in her progress.

The change in her becomes obvious in the way she now responds to her demands of her new situation, especially regarding the new man in her life. Her 'Indian' ways attract Chand Malhotra enough to make him believe he has fallen in love with her, while they endear her to his mother, who is further enamoured of Sinara's invented diplomatic background. When the matchmaking mama requires details of her family, Sinara understands that her real identity will soon be discovered. Though she is tempted, marriage is, however, no longer her sole aim or option. Fortune, too, is on her side now that she is stronger. She writes to Mrs. Graham for help instead of taking the line of least resistance. Elsie-Nora's godmother, lonely and uncomfortable in England, sends for her, and the old racial dream of living there forever is within her grasp at last. She leaves for Home immediately, embarking on the second stage of her journey, fully aware that by returning to her old self she has to give up the sense of belonging to the majority that she has known for the first and last time: "She was going to England to which she owed part of her being but which had not shaped her in any sense that ultimately matters. She was well aware . . . that she was once more going to be the alien." (137) Alienation is the inevitable lot of the nowhere women everywhere.

Mrs. Graham, moreover, is a bitter and lonely woman who demands from her goddaughter the kind of service her Indian servants had given her. She clings on the Elsie-Nora and refuses to let her make a life for herself by marrying a fellow Anglo-Indian who had emigrated to England before Independence. Unlike Mrs. Graham's sons, Hugh Walker has remained as dutiful to his widowed mother as the traditional Indian; but both mother-figures detest each other, all the more so because the romance between the two lonely young Anglo-Indians is a threat to their own security and sense of self. (143) It is only when both the old ladies die that the now middle-aged pair of lovers can marry. By doing so, they realize that they have "come full circle," for, as Elsie-Nora sees it, "I attempted to be Indian, had hoped to be English, had come Home and now returned to my Anglo-Indian roots by marrying Hughie." (146) Now she need strive no longer "to be either one thing or the other. . . . 'I can be myself,' she says, 'whatever I perceive that to be.'" (150)

Elsie-Nora's equilibrium brings about the narrator's own. She realizes that she does not need to know India nor resent her stepfather in her quest for identity. She sees that behind her grandmother's uneasiness about her lies a real concern for a loved one, albeit expressed with typical British understatement and evasion. In her response to her grandmother's offer of cups of tea—"I suppose I must be British after all"—lies the crux of the novel: the nowhere woman can in fact become a person with a self and a place of her own.

NOTES

1. Manorama Mathai, *Mulligatawny Soup* (New Delhi: Penguin, 1993).
2. Juliet Mitchell, "Femininity, Narrative and Psychoanalysis," in *Modern Criticism and Theory: A Reader*, ed. David Lodge (London: Longman, 1988), pp. 426-27.
3. Annis Pratt, *Archetypal Patterns in Women's Fiction* (Bloom-

ington: Indiana University Press, 1981), p. 14.

4. Sandra M. Gilbert and Susan Gubar, *The Madwoman in the Attic: The Woman Writer and the Nineteenth-Century Literary Imagination* (New Haven: Yale University Press, 1979), p. 284.
5. Margaret Atwood, *Survival: A Thematic Guide to Canadian Literature* (Toronto: House of Anansi Press, 1972), p. 36.
7. Jerome H. Buckley, *Season of Youth: The Bildungsroman from Dickens to Golding* (Cambridge, Mass.: Harvard University Press, 1974), pp. 17-18.

"An Aesthetic of Dislocation": Meena Alexander

NEERJA CHAND

Asian American literature is generally defined as literary works written by people of Asian descent who were either born in or who have migrated to North America. This body of literature has undergone dramatic changes ever since it emerged as a distinctive field in the wake of the civil rights movement in the late 1960s more than three decades ago. In recent times, there is a visible shift in focus in this area and whereas identity politics, with its emphasis on cultural nationalism and American nativity, governed theoretical and critical formulations in earlier times, the stress at the moment is on heterogeneity, hybridity, exile, dislocation and Diaspora. As a result, the literary canon has moved and shifted from seeking to "claim America" to forging a connection between Asia and Asian America, in the words of King-Kok Cheung from "centering on race and masculinity to revolving around the multiple axes of ethnicity, gender, class and sexuality; from being primarily concerned with social history and communal responsibility to being caught in the quandaries and possibilities of postmodernism and multiculturalism."[1]

Meena Alexander is one of the recent South Asian American immigrant writers who have emerged and gained from this shift in focus. "A poet and one of the finest thinkers of Asian American aesthetic"[2] in the words of Ketu H. Katrak, Alexander who has lived in New York city since 1980 and teaches English and Creative Writing at Hunter College NY, has published several volumes of poetry and has been widely anthologized in journals both in India and abroad. Having spent a major part of her childhood in Khartoum, Sudan, where she grew up, after being taken there at the age of five and from where she started making annual trips to her grandparents's home in Kerala each summer, Meena is passionately involved with issues like immigration, ethnicity, culture and race relations and focuses in her works on what she calls, in an essay entitled "Is There an Asian American Aesthetics?" "an Aesthetic of Dislocation."[3]

This essay tries to look at some of Alexander's works up to her second novel *Manhattan Music* (1997) in the light of her "aesthetic of dislocation," focusing in particular on the pain and violence of dislocation in her works which is often accompanied by a poetics of loss, as well as emergence of a sensibility enriched by the simultaneity of geography, which involves the possibilities of living here in body and elsewhere in mind and imagination, travelling in Alexander's words "back and forth, forth and back," in a state of suspended animation and inhabiting many different spaces at the same time.

The dislocations and relocations are certainly marked by violence, affecting equally, the artist and the artistic process. The writer says in her essay:

> In India, no one would ask me if I were Asian-American or Asian. Here we are part of a minority, and the vision of being "unselved" comes into our consciousness. It is from this consciousness that I create my work of art. Because of this dialectical element there is a "violence" involved for me even in the production of the work of art. (26)

For Meena Alexander, therefore, the function of the Asian-American artist gets clearly defined. To quote from her essay again:

> For me, in the United States, the barbed wire is taken into the heart and the art of an Asian-American grapples with the disorder in the society, with violence, and in our writing we need to evoke a chaos, a power equal to the injustices that surround us.

The evocation of chaos is the subject matter of the second novel *Manhattan Music* but the "barbed wire," a recurrent motif and metaphor for the pain of negotiating barriers and dislocation, occurs as early as her first book of poems. The poem is entitled "June 1977":

> barbed wire
> drips rust, an engine hoots . . .
>
> Your centuries are brackish, India.
> A black vessel, I
> entirely yours, float
> hull scraping towards her. Barbed
> wire knotting water between us.[4]

The pain and violence of dislocation is the subterranean motif in Meena's first novel *Nampally Road* where the protagonist suffers from dislocation and "comes back to India to have continuity with what she was."[5] Journeying back and forth in time, more recently, *Fault Lines* (1993), her autobiographical memoir, epitomizes a quest wherein the writer plants herself in her early days in Kerala, recounting events from distant childhood, the source of her beginnings. History, myth and memory interact as she recreates strongly felt images of her childhood in Kerala. "The Conch Shell, that seashore, those bellies, that dung"[6] and "the rooms, enfolded each within the other, the distant houses all have held me." (29) As the narrative advances through the gallery of characters, parents are portrayed with fond nostalgia. Amma

> her hands bent into brown shell shapes for the wind to whistle through. She holds up her hands in sunlight, in moonlight. She lifts me high into the wind

and her father who

> stretches out his hands to me. I want to dissolve, become a

> ghost myself, so I can race to my father, into his outstretched hands. (29)

This personal memory dissolves into a universal dilemma of the immigrant travelling through different locations—Allahabad, Tiruvella, Kozencheri, Pune, Khartoum, Cairo—blending with "this other who I am"—in Delhi, London, New York, speaking a multitude of languages: Malyalam, Hindi, Tamil, Arabic, English, French, ending up as a "nowhere creature," questioning herself in an existential manner "Who was I?" In the oft-quoted words from *Fault Lines*:

> Did the ugly Pupa know it would become a butterfly? Where did the butterfly part exist, when the plump thing clung to a leaf in the darkness of a shoe box? Was there some secret that sustained it? Where did my Khartoum life go when I was in Kozencheri or Tiruvella? And what of this life of rock and stone under the thick green leaves of Kerala, when I was living in a desert land so far away? Where was I at any ONE TIME? What was I? (78)

The painful confusion of continuous dislocation is sharpened by the experience of racial hatred and colonization. As the first non-white child at Clergy House School in Khartoum, the writer protagonist undergoes the pangs of the oppressive colonial set up. "My blackness stuck out as a stiff halo around me" (113) a trauma re-enacted years later in America, where as an "unwhite" she is marginalized and addressed strongly as "you black bitch." (169) Earlier in the narrative, she had referred to her first novel as a work that "marks a crossing, a border." Now the sharp edges of the barbed-wire of the border begin to make her ponder philosophically: "Can I make lines supple enough to figure out violence, vent it and pass beyond." (169) The writer-protagonist comes back to her existential dilemma:

> Who are we? What selves can we construct to live by? How shall we mark our space? How shall we cross the

street? How shall we live another day? (174)

The construction and reconstruction of the self is an ongoing process and the violent pain of the "barbed wire" ever present. In a poem published in the volume *Night Scene, The Garden* in the same year as *Fault Lines* (1992), Meena Alexander's invocation to the Muse is expressed in highly charged words

My back against barbed wire
No man's land
no woman's either
I stand in the middle
of my life . . .
Come ferocious alphabets of flesh
splinter and raze my page
That out of the dumb
and bleeding part of me
I may claim
my heritage.[7]

The "ferocious alphabets of flesh" come out strong and the evocation of chaos finds full expression in Meena Alexander's second novel *Manhattan Music* which problematizes the issue of dislocation, its pain and violence and the possibility of relocation and a partial resolution of the immigrant dilemma towards the end. In the story of Sandhya Maria Rosenblum, a Syrian Christian Malayali immigrant in New York, the novel examines the repercussions of migration, the disruption of certitudes and the continual intrusion of memory. All these elements in the novel create and recreate, construct and reconstruct a new and unblemished Sandhya. Through dislocations—physical and psychological, though fragmentation and a fractured psyche, Sandhya finally has an identity which is not totally fragmented or fractured but a reconstructed whole and towards the end of the novel almost relocated and somewhat simplistically, reconciled to her "multiple anchorages."

In *Manhattan Music*, the protagonist Sandhya is initially in an unhappy and confused state of mind. "Nothing felt right," she says.[8] She is also "a black woman married to a white man" (216) and mother of a small daughter Dora, suffering from a growing awareness of the incompleteness of her marriage to Stephen who is totally baffled by her gradual withdrawal, distancing and alienation. To quote:

> Sandhya was growing thinner he could tell, there were circles under her eyes and he sensed something was growing at her. He did not dare ask what outright. What could she have said in any case? (37)

Sandhya's own perception of her situation is summed up in these words:

> The emptiness was growing in her. Something Stephen did not know about and could not touch, a gnawing hunger, a desperation even. (42)

Stephen tries hard to understand and grapple with the situation in order to help Sandhya and also to salvage the relationship. Sandhya looks at her own life with Stephen as a diminished reflection of her husband's. At the same time, she looks critically at Stephen and is also skeptical about "the scope of Stephen's own soul" (9) and looks outside for "a passion that could simplify life." (211) Stephen, on the other hand, tells her that she should take America head on (39) now that she has a Green Card and Dora is safely left in a day care centre.

Sandhya tries to escape from this unhappy situation through dreams of the homeland, Kerala of her childhood and youth. "Barbed wire" reappears as a metaphor, again as a symbol for her disrupted passion for Gautam in India:

> Which had never been consummated and with his death, sexual memory was knotted in her head with the "barbed wire," the Hyderabad police used to torture their victims with. (146)

Sandhya finds a momentary stay against this chaos and confusion in a torrid affair with Rashid el obeid, an Egyptian post-doc Fellow in Columbia who looks Indian "perhaps a Punjabi" (59) but the affair fizzles out because she is searching for much more than temporary escapes and simple distractions. Neither memories of home in India nor an affair with Rashid el obeid whose tumultuous past and cultural history is like her own and who fills her with a longing "to dive in his past, be stung into newness by him" (142) offer any solace to her tormented self. After her break-up with Rashid, Sandhya feels a sudden emptiness in her arms, nothing to hold on to. (56) True, that Stephen offers her a stable and sanitized world but she becomes more and more alienated from it as also she distances herself from Rashid. Stephen, who is comfortably cocooned in his safe status as a first class citizen in white USA does not understand her anxieties and neurosis or those of people like Rashid who come from a similar context but he tries his best to help his wife Sandhya and understand the situation of immigrants in general.

Interestingly, the immigrant is presented in the novel as the monster Frankenstein who, Sandhya recalls, in Mary Shelley's story is a monster made up of bits and pieces of flesh (154) waiting for electricity which would make it come alive. In Rashid's words to Zabir,

> Immigrants are like that—Our spiritual flesh scooped up from here and there. All our memories sizzling. But we need another. Another for the electricity. So we can live. (154)

and

> better to have all the bits than to cleanse, blow up, destroy. For that is the other option, isn't it? A hatred for all the parts of flesh that forms us, wanting the pure blue, the perfect slate. (154)

It is significant to point out that at this stage Sandhya is equally burdened by the unreliability of the past as well as the uncertainty of the future in India and America. When she comes to India on a visit to see her ailing father, Rajiv Gandhi is assassinated in Sriperambedur and communal riots become rampant in India. On the other side of the globe, the Gulf war escalates and religious fanatics contemplate revenge in America. It is chaos everywhere and there is No Exit.

> Totally unable to confront or understand this turbulent world, when even Rashid's love fails to provide any support and certitude from pain, Sandhya breaks down and tries to kill herself with a rope around her neck in her friend Draupadi's flat.

Draupadi, a tough and resilient woman like her namesake in the *Mahabharata*, a second-generation immigrant from the Carribean unlike the new migrant Sandhya, saves her. Inspired by Peter Brooke's *Mahabharata* at BAM, she tells Sandhya:

> We each have to be many women. . . . After all, how many lives did the *Mahabharata* lady have? Crawling through the tunnel to save her life, wasn't she quite different from the princess in the palace? And then the woman bartered in the dice-throw between men, think of her shame, her rage.

But unlike Draupadi, Sandhya cannot retrieve heroism and inspiration from the derogation of history. Her release must originate from "the dark vessel of her past" the load of accumulated past memories that constrict her and hamper her growth as a human being. Sakhi, her cousin takes her to a women's meeting in New York city. As Sandhya sits in the large, ill-ventilated room at Columbia University, among many Asian-American women, Sandhya feels as if she has entered a country where she needed neither a passport nor a green card, nor any other sign of belonging. (211) In the midst of these immigrant women, listening to their woeful testimonies on the platform, Sandhya also begins to "remake her life." In the story of the old woman from Lahore, partly blind in one eye, brought to New York as an Ayah two decades ago, cast out on the streets when she could no longer work, roaming the streets, sleeping on park benches, hiding her face in her dupatta every time she saw a policeman—Sandhya sees reflections of her own life. The story of the younger woman—delicate and well-made, her body buttoned into a dark sweater embroidered with roses—her narration of a violent husband, difficult pregnancy and her flight into the night air, down the cold streets—open up Sandhya's eyes to the diasporic situation of Asian-American women and join them in asking "why should I care?" (212) Very soon Sandhya finds that "There was no way she could turn back the clock, return to Hyderabad," (183) and "she cannot go back. She would stay close to the ground and not be suspended in mid air." (223)

> She was racing into America from the dark vessel of her past and she could hear it singing in her, ready to break free, the load of her womanhood, of the accumulated life, breaking free into an inconceivable sweetness. (219)

Finally, in a chapter significantly entitled *Staying,* Meena Alexander structures Sandhya's reconciliation and relocation, her "electric moment of illumination" and self-realisation when Sandhya "knows that she would live out her life in America" and "Now she couldn't just lean on others. She had to trust herself if she wanted to go on." (226) During a walk in the Central Park, approaching the fence by Harlem Meer where earlier her cousin Jay had drawn her attention to "Manhattan Music," (221) the sounds, subtle as flesh, countless voices (221) singing Asian "Diaspora Ditties," (158) bits of Rock, African dance, Tandava steps woven to the act of dancing. (157) Sandhya finally arrives at her moment of truth. In the Central Park lake, during the mid-morning light, Sandhya watches the emergence of the "dragonfly on the water lily, struggling out of the translucent pupa, large eye coverings left behind in the crumpling skin . . . the new body gleaming with moisture." (227)

Having passed through the purgatorial fire of self-mortification and chaotic near-neurosis, Sandhya experiences a transformation similar to the dragonfly's, the bits and pieces of her flesh coming alive in an electrifying moment, the ugly pupa of *Fault Lines* finally, on the concluding page of *Manhattan Music*, becoming a butterfly:

> she was no longer fearful of the shadows in the trees of the sharp cry of the strange bird with long tail feathers . . . there was a place for her here though what it might be she never could have spelled out. And she who had never trusted words very much, knew she would live out her life in America. (228)

In her negotiation of past and present, Meena Alexander links her protagonist Sandhya's heritage with that of other Asian-Americans. This is a useful strategy of relocation. To quote from her essay:

> I want to find a way that we can make a durable and usable past that is not just nostalgia but exists in the present. The present for me is the present of "multiple anchorages." It is these multiple anchorages that an ethnicity of Asian American provides for me, learning from Japanese Americans, Chinese Americans, African Americans, Indian Americans and everyone juggling, jostling, shifting and sliding the symbols that come out of my mind.

In the same essay, Alexander warns us against "playing with our ethnicity in the post-modernist fashion" as it "is located in our bodies," and not outside it.

For Meena Alexander in the same essay, art is "always political, even if it is most abstract, even if it is simple visual image of a leaf falling from a tree." Dislocation of a leaf from the tree and its multiple transformations in the possibility of becoming a leaf and by extension a tree again, symbolize an immigrant's dilemma. Alexander expresses this dilemma powerfully in a deeply felt "aesthetic of dislocation" that places her protagonist as well as the artist herself, both within ancestral history and in an immigrant relocation in the U.S.A. simultaneously. In doing so, she successfully emerges as a powerful writer whose sensibility is enriched by the simultaneity of geography, which involves the possibilities of living here in body and elsewhere in mind and imagination, inhabiting multiple spaces at the same time.

NOTES

1. King-Kok Cheung, *An Inter-Ethnic Companion to Asian-American Literature* (Cambridge University Press, 1997).
2. Ketu Katrak, "South Asian American Literature" in King-Kok Cheung, p. 206.
3. Meena Alexander, "Is There an Asian American Aesthetics?" *Samar*, 1:26-27, 1992.
4. *Stone Roots* (India: Arnold Heinemann, 1980), p. 21.
5. Meena Alexander, *Nampally Road: A Nove*l (San Francisco, California: Mercury House, 1991), p. 30.
6. Meena Alexander, *Fault Lines: A Memoir* (New York: Feminist Press, 1993), p. 3.
7. Meena Alexander, *Night Scene, The Garden* (New York: Red Dust, 1993), pp. 26-29.
8. Meena Alexander, *Manhattan Music* (San Francisco, California: Mercury House, 1997), p. 7.

Meena Alexander's *Fault Lines*: A Study

D.K. PABBY

In the nineties of the twentieth century, a group of young teachers of English in Delhi University were able to persuade the authorities about the need for changes to be made in English Hons. syllabus of Delhi University. The then Head of the Department wrote letters to all the 600 odd teachers in the 60 old colleges requesting them to participate in this democratic process of revising and updating the syllabus, after a gap of nearly 20 years. In the beginning the debates, in the name of 'opening up the canon' and 'decolonizing English Studies,' turned out to be very turbulent, aggressive, with young friends raising questions about race, gender, class, language, etc. in the selection of the texts. After two or three such long-drawn meetings of the General Body of the teachers of English, a representative-body of one delegate from each college was chosen, and consequently the discussions became more orderly, accommodative and reason-oriented rather than guided by verbose and high-patched battles for inclusion of theory and some new writers from the West. Within smaller groups also, though sharp differences persisted, there was more scope of convincing each other and finally a new syllabus—multicultural and multilingual in content, pluralist in tone and covering as vast a geographical landscape and psychological mindscape as possible—emerged. There is some criticism about the bias for or against some texts: but on the whole the liberality of the new exercise cutting across the Anglo-American mainstream has been widely appreciated. Though a large number of teachers who remained out of touch with what was being written in Indian English and the Bhashas i.e. various national languages of India, did come across some initial, pedagogical problems, it has been generally recognized that this effort is a step in the right direction, to provide a new shift to the English Studies in India, making them more relevant in the context of our cultural ethos which is a part of one's being, acceptability of the diversity of cultural patterns, narrative techniques and poetic-experimentations in different parts of the country. The change, in the beginning, seemed to be a formidable task, but the things are now settling down. Ironically enough, it is the English language which is becoming here, as also in Europe and America, the language of ushering in the process of decolonization, however paradoxical it may seem. Viewed in this light, the writings of South Asian Women immigrant writers, in the West, particularly in North America, acquire added significance. The questions of race, gender, sexuality, cultural differences, multiple identities, engaging their attention in the matter of providing a shift to Multicultural studies, and the result, once again, is inclusion of several texts of variegated cultural experiences and different narrative strategies, making evocative use of the 'memory of the past'—'the roots'—to grapple with the frequent existential self-questionings of—who am I? Whencefrom I come?—and the answers are a bitter-sweet poignant experience of putting 'bits and pieces' together to make a wholesome whole. This is a small contribution to the gigantic task of evolution of multicultural ethos in the wider context of evolving a Western corporate culture giving due respect to 'difference,' 'otherness,' 'femaleness,' 'colour,' 'ethnicity'—in short to pluralism as such. Writings of the poet-novelist Meena Alexander, particularly her memoir, *Fault Lines* (New Delhi: Penguin, 1993), are one of the significant contributions in this direction or process of decolonizing Euro-centric Anglo-American Studies particularly in North America which otherwise provides a congenial democratic environment for 'cross-cultural transactions' wherein the questions of race, gender, ethnicity, etc. get widely discussed and sharply focussed.

Fault Lines, the book by Meena Alexander, an immigrant

Syrian Christian Indian writer, now settled in America, bears a sub-title *A Memoir*. In Webster's *New World Dictionary*, 'Memoir' has been defined as "an autobiography, especially one that is objective and anecdotal rather than inward and subjective, or a report or record of important events based on the writer's personal knowledge or observation." And by author's own admission, the issues of a usable past, of race, gender and self identity, form the subject matter of the fragmented landscapes of this book. (ix) The writer has also submitted that "perhaps some small part of what is imaged here will make sense for them also (for our children Adam and Svati)." (xii) The two epigraphs, one from Kalidasa's *Kumarasambhava* and the other from Franz Fanon's *Black Skins, White Masks*, clarify that Meena Alexander has chosen to articulate her situation of a woman cracked by "multiple migrations," (3) with the help of 'memory,' though she does realize that the house of memory is fragile, make up (as it is) in the mind's space. In the first chapter titled "Fault Lines" she has devoted about half a page to the different meanings of the word "Fault" and has also ruminated as to

> what would it mean for one such as I do pick up a mirror and try to see her face in it?
>
> Night after night, I asked myself the question. What might it mean to look at myself straight—see myself? How many different gazes would that need? And what to do with the crookedness of fresh, thrown back at the eyes? The more I thought about it, the less sense any of it seemed to make. My voice splintered in my ears into a cacophony; whispering cadences, shouts, moans, the quick delight of bodily pleasure, all rising up as if the condition of being fractured had freed the selves jammed into my skin, multiple beings locked into the journeys of one body.
>
> And what of all the cities and small towns and villages I have lived in since birth: Allahabad, Tiruvella, Kozencheri, Pune, Delhi, Hyderabad, all within the boundaries of India; Khartoum, in the Sudan, Nottingham in Britain,

> and now this island of Manhattan? How should I spell out these fragments of a broken geography?
>
> And what of all the languages compacted in my brain: Malayalam, my mother tongue, the language of first speech; Hindi which I learnt as a child; Arabic from my tears in the Sudan—odd shards survive; French, English? How would I map all this in a book of days? After all, my life did not fall into the narratives I had been taught to honour, tales that closed back on themselves, as a snake might, swallowing its own ending; birth, an appropriate education—not too much, not too little—an arranged marriage to a man of suitable birth and background, somewhere within the boundaries of India. (2)

And in response to a question by her friend Roshni; "what are you writing about?" she says; "Writing in search of a homeland. About being born into a female body; about the difficulty of living in space . . . really, living without fixed ground rules, moving about so much, giving birth, about all that." (4)

Thus setting the agenda in the opening chapter, Meena Alexander starts on 'a voyage of self-discovery,' and journeying back and forth in time, surfaces as the essence of the *Fault Lines*. It epitomizes a search wherein the author consciously plants herself in her early childhood days and begins her descriptive portrayal in more or less a chronological order. Starting the story of her life as part of an ancestral past that indirectly shaped her being through her parents George and Mary, she recounts the details about her maternal and paternal grandparents, in the second chapter called 'Mirror of Ink.' Creating a beautiful image of the hands reaching out to the past and present, she writes in lyrical prose:

> To enter the mist, I put out both hands as far as they will reach. My right hand reaches through the mirror with no back, into a ghostly past, a ceaseless atmosphere that shimmers in me even as I live and move. Within it, I feel the warmth of the sun in Tiruvella. I smell the fragrance of

> new mango leaves. My left hand reaches into the present, with it I feel out a space for my living body. I touch rough bricks where the pigeon perched an instant ago, on the wall at the corner of 113th street and Broadway in Manhattan—Turtle island as it once was in a sacred geography. (7)

In this manner, the coalescing of the past and the present goes on throughout the brief narratives in the *Memoir*.

The author reminisces about her infancy years spent in North India, in Allahabad, where her father had his first posting in Independent India. But the visits to Kerala were very regular. In fact, Tiruvella (her maternal grandparents's home) and Kozencheri (her paternal grandparents's home) provide the native ethos as well as the 'red soil' in which she finds the anchor for their physical, mental, religious, spiritual, and social roots. Her sojourns at Pune, Delhi, Hyderabad, Khartoum, Cairo and continual return to Tiruvella and Kozencheri are the variegated experiences, what she calls 'bits and pieces' and which contribute in her echoing recurrent self-questionings: 'Who am I?' 'Where was I at one time? What 'was' I etc. Through the process of groping for clue to herself, the author provides the reader with a clue to her complex identity. She is the philosopher who defines contours of existential states. In the process of growing up, her questions are ponderous and heavy with both 'the mystery and knowledge of the self' as it is transported from one state to another, and from one locale to another.

After early childhood in Allahabad, Pune, and Kerala, there is 'the crossing of borders' to Khartoum days. She receives education, apart from her school, from her parents also. If her father was trying to inculcate in her religious understanding and sentiments, she receives instruction from her mother in the method and art of recognizing herself as a woman: "decorum, perfect, sober dressing, learning the trick of silence, of female invisibility." (106) Womanhood, in its intriguing aspect and stiff demands, posed a formidable challenge for the author in her. The journals written in Khartoum, in the privacy of toilet rooms and nook in the neem-tree, contained within them what she calls "a desperate awareness of my femaleness, a sense of shame." (111)

Viewing herself in a colonial background and having to learn and relearn English in Khartoum, had a tangible effect on her to decolonize linguistically. She experienced the colonial set-up as the first 'non-white child' at the Clergy House School—Khartoum, and felt as she poignantly states: "My blackness struck out like a stiff halo all around me." (113) And even later, during her stint of teaching at Miranda House, Delhi, where she came across important personages and savouring something of the political flavour in the March led by J.P. in 1974, the author discovered more of India, in Delhi. Her association with the Philosopher Society at St. Stephens' College and meeting with Ramu Gandhi in 1974 had a great influence on her, shaping her 'thinking, feeling and being.' However, the question of English and its belongingness in India stayed with her. At times, though she wished to tear herself away from English, she realizes its "sheer force" as a large number of philosophers and writers from various countries and languages were mainly translated into English. Thus despite her awareness of the colonial pressure, she finds herself bound to English in an organic way, as the chief medium of expression. There are sensitive moments in the Memoir when contemplation figures bold and emerges as a statement of philosophy. But the flow of her self-exploration and delineation is passionate and lyrical in its outpourings throughout. Talking about Sarojini Naidu's handling of English Language in the chapter titled "Language and Shame," Meena Alexander writes:

> Reading Naidu's poetry the discourse of her poetry stood at odds with the powerful language of her speeches. . . . I was fascinated by how English worked for her, and how in her political speeches, the language would be turned to the purposes of decolonization. What would it be like if Naidu as a poet had been able to break free of the restrictive ideology that bound her in? What would she have needed in order to make poems of resistance, poems that voiced the body? The questions have not left me. They reverberate in

> my head. (128)

After her marriage to David. Meena Alexander makes another "Continental Crossing" in 1979. As the Memoir moves further into time, the stuff of her evolution and development grows more dense and more complex particularly with her increasing preoccupation with her 'identity and selfhood.' Arriving in America, she carried with her the first draft of her novel *Nampally Road.* The novel bears in its being a special significance as she states: "In my life that work marks a crossing, a border." (159-60) She perceives rather acutely her stepping on to an alien land where the colour of your skin is different,

> you have to explain yourself constantly. It is the confessional thing. Who are you? Where are you from? What do you do? I try to reply. . . . As much as anything else, I am a poet writing in America. But American poet? What sort? Surely not of the Robert Frost or Wallace Stevens variety? An Asian American poet then? Clearly that sounds better. . . . But even there I wonder: Everything that comes to me is hyphenated. (193)

She also seeks refuge in Nampally Road, with all the sheets of paper that formed her novel, she feels "as if having all that papers visible might justify me, a woman without history in this new world." (160) But her experience of being an 'unwhite in America' spells a degree of trauma for her. However, being a sensitive writer saves her from responding and reacting with 'sentimentality.' The experience when the hatred in 'you black bitch' was hurled at her, not only stuns and injures her 'sense of being,' but in the true manner of a creative writer sounds ripples of philosophic thought also through her mind and she ruminates: "Can I make lives supple enough to figure out violence, vent it. and pass beyond?" (169) This stage in *Fault Lines* marks a state of consciousness. in which the author probes deep into her self and strives continuously to know and recognize the reality of an identity. the certainty of a selfhood. and the need and desirability to establish a direct relationship where she belongs, where she has her roots. The feeling of a complex sense of identity reverberates in the author's response to the topic for a symposium: "Writing, Ethnicity, being Other in New York." She writes about an external source invading her person, and eventually one's own self being the wall 'you are driven up' and the 'world's whip' becoming "your own hand holding the thing that is doing the hurting." (190) She responds to the external reality through an interplay of her faculties, impulses, urges, deep-rooted instincts and an awareness of the existence of her femaleness. It is the strongly ingrained tradition and value-system during her formative years in the Kerala that provide her 'up-rooted' and 'exile self in America,' the much-needed anchorage, and her works steeped in that 'red-soil' ethos become markers of her cultural identity.

But as it is, the author in an earnestness must know herself and she scrupulously questions the wherefore of her existence in the perennial 'who am I?' 'Broadway and Manhattan' add to the later concepts of home, but for a belongingness as a creative artist, she has carried with her a geography "a house with a courtyard where I grew up in Tiruvella, my mother's ancestral house with its garden, a single street in front that runs all the way to the old Mar Thomas Church, palm trees, a few buffaloes, ambling in the heat." (197) She feels she is in New York because of what she was in Tiruvella: "And because it was, I am whole and entire. I do not need to think in order to be." (197) Thus her ethnicity as an Asian-American is delineated in an intensity and acuteness of 'self-experience' and a subsequent 'self-expression.' Ethnicity, for her, though at first as a pressure that breaks, essentially resists 'fracturing' and is apprehended by her as the 'perpetual present' always beyond deciphering. My ethnicity as an Indian American, or in broader terms, an Asian American, the gateway it seems to me now to a life in letters, depends upon, indeed requires, a resolute fracturing of self, a splintering of older ways of being. . . . But does this mean that faced with the multiple anchorages, that ethnicity provides, leaving from Japanese Americans, Fillpano Americans, Jewish American, African